PRIMERS FOR PRUDERY

RONALD G. WALTERS

is Assistant Professor of History
at Johns Hopkins University
and is the author of
several articles on America's past.

PRIMERS FOR PRUDERY

Sexual Advice to Victorian America

by

Ronald G. Walters

Prentice-Hall, Inc., Englewood Cliffs, New Jersey

Library of Congress Cataloging in Publication Data

Walters, Ronald G

Primers for prudery.

(A Spectrum Book)

Includes bibliographical references.

1. Sex customs—United States. 2. Family—United States. 3. United States—Moral conditions. I. Title.

HQ18.U5W3 301.41′7973 73-19826

ISBN 0-13-700922-4

ISBN 0-13-700914-3 (pbk.)

A SPECTRUM BOOK

Printed in the United States of America.

10 9 8 7 6 5 4 3 2 1

Prentice-Hall International, Inc. (*London*)
Prentice-Hall of Australia Pty., Ltd. (*Sydney*)
Prentice-Hall of Canada, Ltd. (*Toronto*)
Prentice-Hall of India Private Limited (*New Delhi*)
Prentice-Hall of Japan, Inc. (*Tokyo*)

for Charlotte

CONTENTS

PREFACE

This book is beneficiary of cycles in frankness. During much of this century, topics it touches upon and terminology it reproduces would not have appeared in a work intended for general distribution. Tastes do change and we are at the point where we can again print the words of our staid and proper forbears. Robert Dale Owen, writing in 1830, made the best rebuttal to those who find such open discussion of sexuality offensive. "That chastity which is worth preserving," Owen asserted, "is not the chastity that owes its birth to fear and ignorance" (Robert Dale Owen, *Moral Physiology; Or, a Brief and Plain Treatise on the Population Question* [London: J. Watson, 1841], p. 30).*

The real purpose of this collection is not to assail censorship, nor to flail prudery, nor to appeal to prurient interest, nor even—for that matter—to promote chastity. Those activities could easily be carried out with no reference whatsoever to nineteenth-century pronouncements on sex, love, and marriage. Such pronouncements do, however, serve as an important resource for study of the social aspect of sexuality, which is precisely the reason for gathering together these materials. Sexual expression is not, as we often assume, merely a private and personal matter: history and culture, as well as circumstance and individual psyche, condition erotic behavior and how we regard it.

* This paragraph was written well before a recent Supreme Court decision altered legal standards for judging obscenity. That decision, and much other evidence, indicates that the "cycle of frankness" may now be heading toward less liberal codes of conduct and expression than prevailed in the late 1960s and early 1970s.

Obviously it is difficult to reconstruct historical and cultural features of sexuality—perhaps it is impossible to do so for some time periods and for some social groups; but evidence does survive, including moral and medical literature like that appearing on the following pages.

Yet clearly this literature represents only a beginning. We will ultimately have to have other data and will have to subject it to diverse kinds of analysis before being able to place past sexual attitudes securely in a social context. In the Introduction and within various chapters I do suggest how nineteenth-century American sexual advice might be weighed against actual behavior and against social, legal, demographic, and economic factors. Despite an inevitable tentativeness, a slender volume in an undeveloped field can play its part by making such suggestions, with full awareness that the final word has yet to be spoken, and this collection will have fulfilled its function if it leads to a conviction that comprehension of our ancestors' sexual beliefs and practices is both possible and worthwhile.

Some editorial and stylistic judgments require explanation. Because sexual information appeared in scattered places, not simply in advice books, I have included excerpts from medical treatises, from a manual for homemakers, and from other seemingly peripheral documents. This liberal definition of advice literature has the virtue of conveying a sense of how pervasive certain attitudes were and of how they applied to social, professional, and personal questions. There were, however, other difficulties involved in determining what readings to select, particularly in coping with the problem of overabundance. Hundreds of works giving sexual and marital advice were published in nineteenth-century America, a high proportion of them with relatively equal claims for inclusion here. Yet the literature itself was circumscribed by social and geographic biases and authors did agree on more crucial points than most of them suspected. This rough consensus justified my drawing upon a relatively small sample of authorities, picking those who spoke with reasonable cogency to a wide range of issues. By using these same writers in several different chapters, I sought to give a measure of continuity and to show how individual authors could put sexual concerns into slightly different patterns. In no way would I claim that some of those chosen—John Humphrey Noyes, for instance—should be considered absolutely "representative" of orthodox middle-class morality. Heretics like Noyes are here because even they grew out of a particular culture and were able, in their rebelliousness, to illuminate both the hold of that culture and its failures. It would be futile, I feel, to argue whether any particular nineteenth-century advice-manual author was "typical"—cultural values are quite commonly articulated most clearly by exceptional people. If numbers really do make a difference to critical readers, they can rest assured that virtually all statements made by my two dozen or so writers could be matched by numerous passages not included here.

Still, I do frequently imply a typicality which the evidence does not warrant. From time to time I use terms like "present-day," "twentieth-century," and "nineteenth-century" even though it is patently absurd to imagine that contemporaries ever hold precisely the same beliefs. Connoisseurs of sexual radicalism can find nineteenth-century figures whose behavior and opinions were scarcely "nineteenth-century" in the way I characterize nineteenth-century attitudes. Similarly, chronic browsers in second-hand bookstores will have found twentieth-century health and hygiene tracts asserting ideas I label "nineteenth-century." Terms like "nineteenth-century," "twentieth-century," and "present-day" are a necessary shorthand, made plausible by the fact that at given moments in time there commonly is loose agreement within social groups on central values. Use of this shorthand does not deny cultural continuity across centuries, nor does it deny differences within a particular time period—it simply saves one from continually making minor qualifications to statements when a broad outline is called for. In any case, I have tried in the Introduction to be candid about what and whom advice manual authors may *not* represent, and I recognize that what people state as being desirable does not inevitably describe everyday behavior. Nonetheless, to dwell on deficiencies in a body of source material is to miss its significance; and the following documents, although undoubtedly not descriptive of all nineteenth-century American attitudes, do have something important to say about a portion of our culture and they can be combined with what we know from other sources to produce a deeper understanding of the American past—and present.

Neither footnotes nor bibliography can adequately acknowledge scholarly and personal debts. Several men and women have been generous in allowing me access to unpublished manuscripts and in otherwise sharing insights from their research. I have particularly benefited from the work of Ben Barker-Benfield, Stephen Nissenbaum, Charles and Carroll Rosenberg, and Edward Shorter. Tom and Carol Leonard provided various types of congenial assistance; Carol McKusick, Marc Sober, and Barbara Williams helped immeasurably in the frantic months just before this book was completed. Charlotte Walters was involved with the project from the beginning, reading perceptively both sources and drafts of manuscript. Originally she was to appear as co-editor but contemporary urban ills called her attention from nineteenth-century advice literature. Her contribution, however, transcends that of critic.

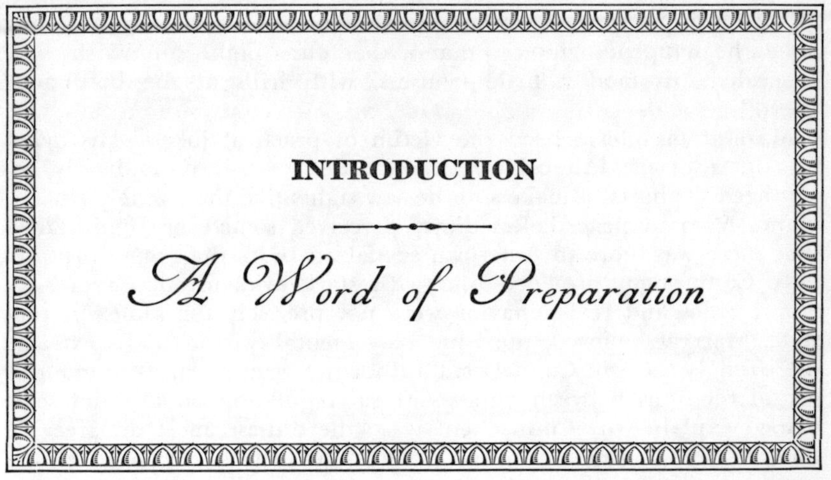

INTRODUCTION

A Word of Preparation

Sex—a characteristic animals possess or an act they engage in, definitely not a topic fit for public conversation. Such is what genteel nineteenth-century Americans must have believed, or so the prevalent image of Victorian prudishness would lead us to think. There is, of course, a measure of truth behind the stereotype of nineteenth-century sexual repressiveness: some of our ancestors did express acute discomfort when confronted with anything erotic. Edward Livingston, a pioneer judicial reformer, omitted certain sexual offenses from a model law code he drafted for the new state of Louisiana, reasoning that a body of laws should be open to the public and "as every crime must be defined, the details of such a definition would inflict a lasting wound on the morals of the people."[1] To talk about sexual transgressions, even for the sake of punishing them, would, in Livingston's view, encourage depravity. (His scruples did not prohibit discussing crimes of violence.) Some nineteenth-century foreign visitors also thought they detected in Americans an especial squeamishness regarding sexual and bodily functions. Captain Frederick Marryat, a worldly English novelist and ex-sailor, was one of those who found American sensitivity remarkable. "They object to everything nude in statuary," Marryat complained, slyly pointing out that Americans "forget that very often in the covering and the covering only, consists the indecency. . . ." Marryat further cited the example of a girl whose modesty was so highly developed that she was deeply offended when he used the word "leg" to refer to the "limb" she injured in a fall.

He later discovered Americans who, to his astonishment, felt that legs were risqué even on musical instruments. In a seminary for young ladies he happened upon a piano, the four "limbs" of which were concealed "in modest little trousers, with frills at the bottom of them!"

Marryat may have been the victim of practical jokers. His belief in American prudishness was ill-concealed and it undoubtedly encouraged his hosts to make sure he saw sights like the chastely clothed piano. Marryat nevertheless dimly perceived something significant—that there was more to American sexual attitudes than mere prudishness. Connecticut provided him with stark evidence that repressive moral codes and real behavior were not precisely the same. In that state, Marryat believed, the Blue Law mentality reached its extreme (he wrongly thought Connecticut authorities went so far as to monitor sexual relations between horses). Moral regulation on a grand scale helped explain why Connecticut was "the dullest, most disagreeable state in the Union. . . ." Yet private conduct hardly justified the public sanctimoniousness he found there. According to Marryat, "so far from the morals of the community being kept uncontaminated by this rigour, the very reverse is the case—especially as respects the college students [at Yale], who are in the secret practice of more vice than is to be found in any other establishment of the kind in the Union." [2] Connecticut may or may not have been preeminent in dullness, and Yale may or may not have been preeminent in licentiousness, but Marryat had begun to grasp a national anomaly: public suppression of sensuality in America mingled with flagrant expressions of it. Some nineteenth-century men and women displayed horror at nudity in statues, and saw indecency in the human (or piano) leg, but others of them tampered with conventional marital arrangements in groups like the Mormons, established notorious houses of prostitution, and produced impressive quantities of pornography.

There is a puzzle here, bits and pieces of feeling, thought, and behavior which are alien to us but which deserve to be put back together in an understandable way. Fortunately—because it makes the process of reconstruction much easier—Americans *did* carry on a public discourse about sex and related matters, although often with maddening delicacy and romantic vagueness. The discourse assumed great vigor in the 1830s and has continued to the present day, despite a rash of restrictive legislation in the 1870s. From the early years of the last century onward, ministers, doctors, quacks, and laymen of one sort or another have eagerly assumed the burden of counseling Americans about sex, sex roles, and allied topics.

Yet the fact that old advice manuals exist does not guarantee that the evidence they contain relates to anything particularly worth knowing. History traditionally has dealt with political, diplomatic, military, and economic events, and it is reasonable to ask whether there really is any importance to what people long dead thought about sex, or any importance to their sexual behavior generally. Those historical works which do speak of erotic matters often do so in two quite different ways, neither of which is likely to resolve doubts about the significance of viewing past sexual expression. On one hand there has been something of a gossip-column approach, dwelling on licentiousness and taking inordinate interest in uncommon individuals, in the amours, paramours, and frustrated amours of great men and women. Heroes, heroines, and villains are never more fascinating than when burning with passion (or otherwise suffering its consequences). In a few cases such sexual adventures may be a legitimate item of concern, reflecting or affecting a public figure's style of leadership; and in some instances events may have taken the shape they did because a prominent person acted out of lust, jealousy, or romantic pique—Henry VIII's marital escapades, for instance, had political repercussions. Such cases, nevertheless, are rare and belong more to remote than to modern times: in an era of total war no face is capable of launching a thousand ships. On the other hand, some writers have chosen to discuss past sexuality with little reference to individuals. Herbert Marcuse and Norman O. Brown, most notably, have constructed elaborate dialectics with Eros as a driving force, moving through the ages.[3] Insightful as these approaches can be, they frequently are prophecy rather than history, using the past as a means to construct a vision of a nonrepressive future. Furthermore, grand schemes like Brown's, in which sexuality and death duel for mastery across centuries, help us perceive things about the human condition, but only at such a high level of abstraction that we cannot explain specific historical events. After reading Brown and Marcuse we may have a better understanding of why many people in the Western world are unhappy, but we are no closer to comprehending particular phenomena like the sudden emergence of birth control literature after 1830.

At one extreme, then, scholars have not been able to see the significance of sexuality through all the erotic trivia of individual lives; at the other extreme, they have not been able to grasp the detail behind Eros' cosmic significance. Only a few historians have found a promising middle way, placing sexual attitudes and activity amidst other social concerns. Among Americans who have done this, David Brion Davis has traced the violent interplay between erotic impulses and homicide in pre–Civil War fiction; and Winthrop D. Jordan, searching out the origins of American racial attitudes, has charted complex connections between sexuality, Anglo-American culture, and a wealth of other factors.[4] Despite these important exceptions, there has been little work to integrate sexual attitudes and activity with larger interpretations of particular time periods and with theories of cultural change—and that is exactly what must be done to give analysis of past sexuality its place as a legitimate part of historical study. When sexual attitudes and activities are put in a more general context, as Davis, Jordan, and some others have begun to do, the results are impressive. We acquire a richer understanding of our forbears' thought and behavior; and we gain an appreciation for the manner in which history and culture have modified sexual expressiveness.

There is, after all, an historical dimension to sexuality. Evolution emancipated human beings from some hormonal and instinctual controls found among lower animals; the cortex of the brain, in addition to glands and environment, guides man's erotic activity. The result, according to one psychologist, is that "much of human sexuality depends upon what the individual *thinks* rather than what is biologically so" [5]—and what men and women have thought about sex and relations between the sexes has varied in time and from culture to culture. Anthropological studies reveal a fascinating range of ways in which humans have structured erotic drives, family patterns, and roles assumed by males and females. What we conceive of as masculine or feminine behavior would appear to be its opposite—or just plain ridiculous—to many other peoples; what we assume to be normal sexual conduct would seem perverse or licentious or unnecessarily prudish.[6] Even if the erotic impulse itself is buried in human biology, diverse societies have found, it seems, any number of forms allowing men and women to satisfy it. Consequently, the manner in which societies (including our own) organize reproduction and deflect or define erotic impulses is as much a part of their particular past, present, and future as the way they organize, deflect, and define economic activity.

The problem is that we write history from whatever sources we have at hand and sexual attitudes and activities are far more private, suppressed, and removed from consciousness than are obviously public kinds of endeavor. For the past especially, it takes a good deal of effort to track down erotic impulses and their effects; by contrast, evidence of political and economic developments is usually accessible and capable of more precise analysis: scholars can try to measure growth of industrialization and formation of political parties, but no one has yet found how to quantify sexual repression. Add to such methodological difficulties the traditional assumption that sexuality is irrelevant to the world of social change and the result is almost total ignorance of one of man's deepest urges in its historical settings.

Yet the ignorance is largely willful. Evidence on past sexual beliefs and actions does exist—laws and criminal court records give social norms and deviations from them; population trends say much about patterns of marriage, reproduction, and illegitimacy; letters and diaries allow glimpses into relationships between individuals; and there are, from the nineteenth century, volumes of public pronouncements about sex of the kind reprinted here. These sources are not absolutely self-interpreting and they must continually be put into relationship with other aspects of the larger culture, including things which are not overtly sexual; but, if used properly, the documents are quite revealing of ties between man's erotic impulses and the social structure with which he surrounds himself. The rich vein of nineteenth-century advice literature, for example, by its very presence points to changes occurring in basic institutions: such literature was necessary because church and family could no longer be relied upon adequately to indoctrinate men and women in proper morality.

Various other forms of expression similarly manifested sexual attitudes. Without knowledge of nineteenth-century sexual morality it is difficult to recapture the mentality behind American literature of the time, in which eroticism frequently became a metaphor for disintegration and a prelude to destruction. Without a sense of orthodox morality it is hard to comprehend why so many nineteenth-century people strove frantically to rearrange relations between the sexes: why the Woman's Rights movement, arising in the 1830s, protested the lustful tyranny of males; why Shakerism, with its enforced celibacy, vied for converts with Mormonism, which encouraged polygamy, and with communitarian societies like Oneida, which allowed "complex marriage" and made intercourse a matter for community discussion. It would similarly be impossible to unravel the diverse forces behind early birth control literature and behind attempts to "perfect the race" through guided reproduction. Without an assessment of sexual attitudes, many passions of articulate Americans would be incomprehensible—among them a fear whites felt for the potency of black people and immigrants, and an anxiety among reformers over licentiousness in America's burgeoning cities.

Sexual concerns inevitably had their most direct effect within the family—the social mechanism responsible for regulation of erotic drives. Indeed, nineteenth-century American families, particularly those of the middle class, betrayed stresses which were largely economic and social, but which also proceeded in fine interaction with sexual behavior and sex roles. As the economy became more complex, families manufactured fewer goods in the home, sending working husbands out of the house for long hours and sharpening a distinction between the world of family and the world of work. Consequently, the home increasingly became woman's domain, although for intelligent and energetic women it could be frustratingly confined, surrounded as it was by a bustling and exciting male-dominated society. Heightened economic and social differentiation between the sexes fostered a feeling that there were equally great innate spiritual and psychological differences separating them: men were assumed to be calculating, aggressive, and sexual; women were thought to be warmly emotional, passive, and asexual. These were not necessarily "natural" roles and they represented some modifications of earlier American concepts of masculinity and femininity; but these idealized images justified changes in nineteenth-century family structure (telling men they belonged outside the home and women they belonged within it) and formed a background for changes in prescribed codes of conduct between male and female, including the sexual conduct advocated in advice manuals.

Admittedly, we are back to the problem of finding evidence. Much of what transpired in courtship and in the household is lost. We cannot recapture whispered words, meaningful glances, or secret acts; but there are indirect indications of real alterations in nineteenth-century marital sexual behavior, alterations corresponding to those preached in moral tracts. The American birth rate, for example, dropped steadily and markedly throughout the century, having been at its all-time high around 1800, an especially striking decline since the percent of women in childbearing years actually increased. By 1840 American mothers could, on the average, expect to have in their lifetimes one less child than their grandmothers had had forty years earlier.[7] Because there were no biological or environmental factors adequate to explain shifting American birth patterns, it seems probable that deliberate modification of sexual behavior produced what was a trend of major social importance, a tendency toward smaller families. Contraception undoubtedly played its part, with books, pamphlets, and advertisements describing various techniques emerging after 1830.[8] Birth control literature, however, followed three decades of declining birth rates and may well only have justified and reinforced what was already established. Most likely, decreasing family size was a tribute both to contraceptive practices and to the stringent sexual morality demanded by a majority of authorities, including those most opposed to birth control. Advice literature offered couples two alternatives: birth control publicists stressed early marriage and contraception while other writers advocated late marriage, intercourse primarily for reproduction, and reproduction only at infrequent intervals. In either case the result would be the same—fewer children.

Assumptions about sexual activity also permeated institutions other than the family. Nineteenth-century insane asylums contained numerous human beings whose misfortunes were credited to masturbation or sexual "excess." Medical writers attributed a remarkable variety of ailments to erotic activity and at times regarded sex itself as a form of pathology.[9] American education similarly felt the icy touch of men and women engaged in battle to contain and control sexuality. There was a movement afoot, particularly after 1850, to institute physical training as a part of curriculum, ostensibly an innocent enough desire. But among its prophets were men like Dio Lewis, who set up an influential school of "light gymnastics" in Boston in 1860. Lewis's own bearish view of sexuality was captured graphically by a section title in a book of his on *Chastity*: "LASCIVIOUS DAY-DREAMS A RANK POISON." Lewis and his fellows believed, as one of them put it, that "a vigorous life . . . not only does not tend to sensuality in the objectionable sense, but it helps avert it." [10] Too much study enfeebled the body, drained off vital energies, and simultaneously managed to encourage erotic thought; only a proper course of exertion could restore balance and virtue, or so Lewis and his colleagues believed. This is not to say that there was nothing more to the movement for physical education than a desire to control eroticism. Few people would now want to abolish exercise and play for students. Nevertheless, this major change in secondary school and college curriculum drew upon a sense that by perfecting (and fatiguing) the body, "unhealthy" sensuality could be prevented.[11]

Moral pronouncements, however, aim at the individual, and there is a question of what happened to those exposed to nineteenth-century sexual advice. Because would-be moral guides were not always agreed among themselves, there was room to pick and choose what one might believe; in addition, humans find it possible to know ethical codes and to ignore them anyway. Yet the dominant note of nineteenth-century orthodoxy was sexual restraint and we do have good evidence of people following anti-erotic prescriptions in public (and sometimes private) life. It would, furthermore, be a mistake to imagine that such moral heroes were mere misfits, atypical men and women so sexlessly neurotic as to be defective in all social relationships. Unwholesome as nineteenth-century standards appear by present-day wisdom, they did secure loyalty from human beings who were active, productive, and respected. Godfrey Lowell Cabot, born in 1861, became as obnoxiously proper a Bostonian as existed, a leading light in the smut-hunting Watch and Ward Society and otherwise totally committed to stamping out public licentiousness. Although Cabot was capable of expressing sexual passion for his wife (to a degree she eventually found distressing), the couple never intentionally viewed each other's naked bodies throughout their many years of marriage, and Cabot took the precaution of writing sensuous passages in letters to her in a foreign language, as if English prose were too pure to bear his message. Cabot, irascible and unlovable, a mixture of prudishness and prurience, was nevertheless a well-functioning member of his society and an aggressively prosperous businessman.[12]

It is tempting to explain the very success of a man like Cabot in terms of erotic impulses channeled into other kinds of activity—sexuality sublimated by command of a harsh morality, transferred into a passion for work and entrepreneurship. Making the connection more alluring, there were obvious parallels between sexual orthodoxy and nineteenth-century economic dogma, with (for example) continence being an equivalent of thrift.[13] Even the metaphors of business and sex had a certain interchangeability: "to spend" was a common slang term for ejaculation. The danger here, as in so many psychological interpretations, is of claiming too much. Men undoubtedly did express erotic impulses in economic activity, as happens today; and nineteenth-century sexual attitudes thoroughly encouraged people to divert sexual impulses into rigorously respectable pursuits. But there were exceptions—entrepreneurs like Jim Fisk who spent all their resources freely—and it simply will not do to portray capitalism as a product of sexual repression or, conversely, to depict sexual repression as a product of nineteenth-century capitalism. Instead, there was a mutual reinforcement between sexual ethics and economic life; they complemented each other—interacted—and both of them were significant parts of the larger structure of American society.

Men like Godfrey Cabot were the success stories of nineteenth-century morality. There were also failures, men and women obsessed with guilt over actions they committed or urges they possessed, especially so because authorities forecast dire physical and divine punishment for sexual transgressions. At this point the orthodox code not only formed individual personality in a destructive fashion, it also helped manufacture one of the weapons of its own ruin. Freudian psychology, arriving in America as the century closed, partly derived from orthodox morality—presenting its acute effects, particularly repression and sublimation of sexual desire, as eternal principles of man's nature. Yet in its therapeutic functions Freudian psychology sought to heal wounds inflicted by that morality, to cure disorders suffered by men and women who could not reconcile erotic drives with their anti-erotic upbringing—to provide a resolution between human desires and pressures generated by a restrictive culture. The first Americans seeking psychiatric aid, according to Nathan Hale, Jr., frequently "had been raised in deeply religious families by strict, puritanical mothers, some of whom had instructed their children in the sexual hygiene of 'civilized' morality."[14] Here are perhaps the surest signs of the prevalence of an unbending sexual code: the number of people who clung to it firmly enough to have their lives disturbed by it; the enthusiasm with which Freudianism was greeted in America; and, since the end of the nineteenth century, a persistent identification of freedom from sexual taboos with assault on the traditional social order—an acknowledgment that respectability and sexual restraint go together.

In a variety of ways, then, sexual morality, attitudes, and behavior permeated nineteenth-century American culture, intersecting dissimilar forces and subtly helping shape institutions as well as people. This is not to say that sexuality was the *cause* of nineteenth-century American development; yet sexual attitudes, themselves products of a particular time and place, did weave in and out of other concerns, giving importance to certain kinds of issues, and permitting men and women to see themselves and the world about them in a particular fashion. We still need a means of coherently integrating study of man's erotic urges into a greater historical framework; but contact with this sampling of nineteenth-century documents may stir readers to refine or reject the suggestions I have made, and, more important, to uncover additional ways in which sexuality and sexual morality have influenced actions and perceptions in the past.

❧

The legitimacy of studying the history of human sexuality is one thing; making sure one has the right materials to do so is another. Even a person favorably disposed to the topic might well question the limits imposed on this collection, which consists of excerpts drawn from advice books and from a scattering of related documents likewise conveying assumptions about desirable sexual behavior.

There is, first of all, a problem of geography—of whether it is correct to take sources from only one nation. Many ideas promoted by Americans were not uniquely American; they echoed European medical literature and sexual lore. To be sure, some authors prided themselves on their national chauvinism and ignorance of European writings. Sylvester Graham, denying cribbing from the British, congratulated himself because "it is nearly twenty years since I have read any work on intellectual and moral philosophy." [15] Nonetheless, Graham's sexual pronouncements, and the dietary rules for which he is better known, were not so very different from ideas proclaimed across the Atlantic. Americans better read than Graham time and again quoted Europeans like Samuel Tissot, an eighteenth-century Swiss physician who believed sexual "excess" destroyed good health. An international survey of sexual attitudes and behavior would be extremely useful, a means of checking transmission of values and a chance to see if different cultures caught in economic processes like industrialization responded similarly or dissimilarly.[16]

Still, there are good reasons for dealing only with America. Although beliefs, and even some demographic trends, cut across national lines, they took different form in different places. American attitudes toward marriage and population expansion inevitably had to accommodate to our social fluidity and abundance of open land, both of which encouraged mobility and early wedlock. Sexual orthodoxy in this country also had to contend with peculiar social and environmental conditions making possible communal societies like Oneida and religious sects like the Mormons, both blatantly defiant of public standards. In addition, America's large black and immigrant populations presented opportunities for a particular kind of lurid sexual imagination. Some native-born white Americans not only fretted about promiscuity among the lower orders and the very rich (as did some Europeans), they also dwelt upon the supposed licentiousness of black people and foreigners. Special circumstances in American life, then, made for special patterns of sexual belief and activity—worth considering in relative isolation from developments elsewhere.

There is nothing so sharp as a national border to mark off a proper span of time to study. Sexual attitudes do not change with the dramatic obviousness of a war or a depression; they are often subtle, private, and imprecisely dated. Although we speak of a general culture, or of prevalent attitudes, there are always exceptions: people of varying ages, experiences, upbringings, and beliefs all alive at the same moment. Nothing can be done but to recognize that any way of singling out a few decades is bound to be arbitrary. Some ways, nevertheless, are not so arbitrary as others. There does appear to have been a striking transformation in sexual awareness after 1830; the tone of gloom in published materials deepened, with restrictiveness replacing relatively more relaxed attitudes. This is particularly fascinating because much of the medical literature supporting the new sexual consciousness existed long before the 1830s. Translations of Tissot appeared in America more than a half-century earlier, and Benjamin Rush's important treatise on insanity, partly reprinted in this collection, presented the case against sexual "excess" decades before a flood of cautionary literature carried it to the masses after 1830. And yet the 1830s do appear to mark a beginning point of sorts, a time when people began increasingly to see sex and sexual behavior as things to be watched and controlled far more closely than they had been in the eighteenth century.[17] The reasons for such a change are more obscure than the change itself, although I suspect that the best explanation is in anxieties middle-class Americans felt about their rapidly transforming nation and its potential for moral disintegration.

A decade to stop with is even less apparent than a starting point, although significant developments did occur toward the end of the nineteenth century. By then challenges were out to orthodox morality: political and sexual radicals disdained it while psychological and medical theory had come to question some of its scientific rationale. At the same time, forces representing traditional virtue attempted to close off debate. In both America and England anti–vice crusades took hold, counting among their casualties serious discussion of sex as well as distribution of contraceptive literature and materials. From the 1870s onward, armies of suppression, energetically led in America by Anthony Comstock, managed to have activities and publications which would have passed through in previous years suddenly declared illegal. There were grim ironies here; in Britain, for instance, a famous trial for distribution of birth control literature involved a book first written and printed by an American doctor four decades before. As orthodox sexual morality tottered into decrepitude it prohibited what it had tolerated in days of greater vigor.[18] Because Comstock laws made rational discourse more difficult, and because Freudianism changed the direction of sexual theory not long after, this collection considers nothing written more recently than the mid-1880s; older attitudes and patterns did persist, but amidst alterations and stresses that deserve consideration at more length elsewhere.

Any sampling of advice literature, whatever its territorial or chronological range, is bound to suffer other limitations, some of them in the nature of the material. Published sources do not necessarily reflect private behavior; they describe ideals rather than reality. Personal papers, by way of contrast, do allow some insight into behavior and are the historian's poor equivalent to the psychoanalyst's verbal probing of his subject's inner life. I have, however, resisted a temptation to include personal papers here because they do not convey the sense of social values to be gathered from books and pamphlets, which were designed to move or to confirm public opinion. Although a sex manual tells nothing about how particular individuals behaved, it can tell a great deal about how moralists believed individuals ought to act, and it can place sex in its network of cultural norms far more successfully than even an extremely revealing diary could.

Probably the most disturbing limitation on nineteenth-century advice literature lies in the kinds of people who wrote it. All the usual American social biases appear. Among the groups underrepresented, or entirely absent, are women, black people, Jews, Catholics, immigrants, the indigent, and professed homosexuals. There is even sectional prejudice, with little appearing from the South, Midwest, South-west, Northwest, or Far West. Some of the exclusions were innate to nineteenth-century morality. Homosexuality, for instance, was thought to be unspeakable, and it rarely appears even as a problem in orthodox literature. Laboring under ferocious pressures toward suppression, homosexuals could feel little else besides guilt and shame, or could expect nothing better than derision if they were brave enough to step forth. Underrepresentation of women likewise was a function of sexual morality. The nineteenth century produced many female authors who addressed themselves to health and hygiene; yet they usually had the delicacy to confine themselves to "feminine" problems and, because women were thought to be less sexual than men, there was presumably less sexual information to dispense. An advice book addressed to young ladies could reasonably omit the lectures against masturbation and licentiousness which characterized similar books addressed to young men. No doubt there were young ladies badly in need of admonition, just as doubtless there were homosexuals, Jews, Catholics, immigrants, poor people, blacks, and non-Easterners who had sexual information worth printing. Still, writing advice books, like other important forms of endeavor in nineteenth-century America, was a job reserved for native-born white heterosexual males of Northeastern Protestant stock.

We can only wonder what those who did not write advice books would have said; by the century's end many of the most dreadful mutterings were directed at them, at promiscuity and prolific reproduction among immigrants and other purportedly "inferior" people. It is not certain, however, that the inarticulate would have put into words values diametrically opposed to those that were expressed, once racial, ethnic, and class slurs were subtracted—perhaps so, perhaps not. My own suspicion is that knowledge of orthodox moral codes and medical beliefs was widespread, even though obedience to the codes was not absolute. Sexual restraint of the sort promoted time and again in the literature provided a standard of respectability by which to measure one's own successes and failures, achievements and guilt—a standard available to all classes, if only as a reproach to some of them for their sins. Americans seeking help from early Freudians seem to have come from a broader social spectrum than had Freud's European clients—probably due to thorough diffusion of fearsomely demanding ideas about sexual control.[19] Testimonials reprinted in advice books likewise came from humble people as well as from the middle-class.

Even so, there is cause to be suspicious of advice manual authors, the odd assortment of doctors, ministers, and rank amateurs who poured forth their prose upon the nineteenth-century reading public.[20] Among their number were strange men like Sylvester Graham, forever associated with his unappetizing bread (miraculously transformed into the present-day Graham cracker); proper diet, Graham thought, cured all maladies, including sensuality. Swedenborgian advisers drifted off into transcendental rhapsodies about relations between male and female; water-cure advocates, meanwhile, urged imaginative ways of using water to fill and cleanse the body for purity's sake; phrenologists, on the other hand, believed they could determine who should reproduce and whose lust was potentially ungovernable by scrutinizing configurations of skulls. Surely people with such bizarre ideas must have been cranks, representative of nothing other than gullibility. Some of them were, but fewer than one might expect; mixed in with the cranks were respected medical men. More to the point, cranks and respected medical men were not easily distinguishable by their sexual beliefs. They often agreed on important matters like the physical and mental effects of "excess," and they even agreed on some of the "cures" most contrary to contemporary practice. Absurd as Graham and his dietary ideas were, for instance, quite sober physicians felt as Graham did that certain foods inspired lust while others curbed licentious tendencies.[21]

Many other seemingly crankish features of nineteenth-century sex manuals gained wide credibility in their own day, ultimately blended into later beliefs and practices of physicians and social scientists, and deserve more respect than we might initially be inclined to give them. Some marginal figures whose theories would fail to pass the muster of present-day standards received high honor in their lifetimes, or shortly after. Dio Lewis, a doctor more by courtesy than qualification, rated favorable mention for his gymnastics program in early histories of physical education in schools. His stout defense of *Chastity* called forth praise from distinguished people like Moses Coit Tyler, a literary historian of note, who thought Lewis's discussion to be "frank and noble-minded."[22] The pseudo-sciences also had surprising vitality. Phrenology may not have been able to forecast a man's amativeness by classification of his head, but its measurements turned up in early academic anthropology and were used for correlations with intelligence well into this century.[23] Similarly durable was the impact of misinformation about prenatal influences on human development, claims that circumstances like a mother's mood at the time of conception or a father's moral character would be indelibly impressed upon the fetus. Later discredited, such beliefs nevertheless marked the beginning of scientific hereditarian thought in America and prepared the way for popular acceptance of Darwinism. By the end of the nineteenth century, ideas resembling these re-emerged in the eugenics movement, which drew many prominent Americans to its program of encouraging only the supposedly most desirable types of people to reproduce.[24] Some caution, then, is necessary before dismissing ideas contained in nineteenth-century advice manuals. Any single assumption may well have been more prevalent than the author's whole program, and the idea in question could well be an ancestor to a body of popular or scientific knowledge worthy of greater attention.

No matter how influential, respectable, or characteristic the sexual advice conveyed in nineteenth-century manuals was, we still have an easy time marking the distance between it and our own conventional wisdom. An authority in the 1880s could write forbiddingly about "excessive venery." The 1960s, however, ended with *The Sensuous Woman* and the 1970s had scarcely begun before we were up to *The Sensuous Couple,* with higher numbers and more exotic combinations scheduled to appear.[25] Our ancestors would have been horrified.

Yet there is an injustice to nineteenth-century men and women in imagining they were less enlightened than we. They were not all frigid old maids and pious hypocrites who preached abstinence while thinking dirty thoughts. That image has its grain of truth, but there is a great deal more to be said. These were men and women who, despite their sexual quirks (by present-day standards), had uncommon vision, courage, and energy—possibly because they suppressed erotic impulses, but virtues commanding respect whatever their origin. The Godfrey Cabots were, after all, shapers and builders of a dynamic society. Furthermore, human sexuality is modifiable and there is no need to assume people in nineteenth-century America were wretchedly miserable because their sexual code ran counter to all but the most conservative present-day preachings. Men and women who fully accepted the terms of nineteenth-century ethics did find personal contentment and satisfaction in well-regulated relationships with the opposite sex. Among the papers of American reformers professing strict morality there are moving examples of warmly affectionate husbands and wives.[26] Nineteenth-century sexual beliefs did severely condemn those who deviated from prescribed behavior and did produce psychological dislocations (Freudianism testifies to that); but restrictive codes could not have survived as long as they did had they been utterly inappropriate to the lives of large numbers of people.

In further defense of nineteenth-century attitudes, advice manuals were not antisexual in any simple manner. Although reiterating the need for restraint, control, and continence, they in some respects placed a higher value on erotic activity than writers would in the mid-twentieth-century. Sex, put under rational guidance, might well save the world, nineteenth-century authorities hinted. Through sexual control came elevation of the human spirit—true civilization—and through intelligent procreation would come a better, more prosperous race of human beings. Reproduction had its spiritual elements as well as its potential dangers in nineteenth-century literature. Intercourse was an act of almost cosmic significance rather than the enjoyable and harmless avocation it sometimes seems to be in contemporary advice books. Erotic activity was part of a web of personal and social considerations, not a private pastime.

Sanctimoniousness comes easily; it came easily in the nineteenth century when erotic offenders were caught and it comes easily when the twentieth century judges the nineteenth. Yet we should make no extreme claims for enlightenment about sex. Old myths persist, even in places where they could be expected to have vanished long ago. A survey taken in 1959 of future doctors graduating from Philadelphia area medical schools revealed that about half of those questioned still held the discredited idea that masturbation is a common cause of insanity. More appalling, about twenty percent of the medical school faculty polled shared the belief. In 1966 the *Journal of the American Medical Association,* praising the pioneering sexual research of William Masters and Virginia Johnson, added a sad commentary on the state of professional wisdom. "Perhaps one reason why many physicians have abdicated their role in providing sexual advice is recognition that their knowledge is deficient," wrote the editors.[27]

Some progress has been made. Those who deviate from sexual norms, although still punished, suffer fewer disabilities than in the past; and basic knowledge of the human reproductive system has improved since the nineteenth century, when authorities were frequently dead wrong on such crucial matters as the point in the menstrual cycle at which women are capable of conception. Yet the reading public's continuing hunger for sexual advice, the persistence of sexually caused psychological disorders, and other even less lovely phenomena of modern life stand as cautionary signs, warning us that we have not outdistanced the nineteenth century as much as we might like to think in our journey to comprehend the darkly mysterious erotic urges within mankind.

---

1 Quoted in David Brion Davis, *Homicide in American Fiction, 1798–1860: A Study in Social Values* (Ithaca: Cornell University Press, 1957), pp. 151–52.

2 Captain [Frederick] Marryat, *A Diary in America, with Remarks upon Its Institutions,* Vol. I (Philadelphia: T. K. & P. G. Collins, 1840), pp. 154, 68.

3 Herbert Marcuse, *Eros and Civilization: A Philosophical Inquiry into Freud* (Boston: The Beacon Press, 1955); and Norman O. Brown, *Life Against*

Death: The Psychoanalytic Meaning of History (1959; reprint, New York: Random House, n.d.).

4 In Davis, *Homicide in American Fiction*; Winthrop D. Jordan, *White Over Black: American Attitudes Toward the Negro, 1550–1812* (Chapel Hill: University of North Carolina Press, 1968).

5 Andrew M. Barclay, "Biopsychological Perspectives on Sexuality," in *Sexuality: A Search for Perspective,* ed. Donald L. Grummon and Andrew M. Barclay, with the assistance of Nancy K. Hammond (New York: Van Nostrand Reinold Company, 1971), p. 62. Note, however, that even in lower animals some aspects of sexual response are learned—animals raised in absolute isolation often do not develop normal sexual expression with their own species.

6 For a fascinating compendium of divergent sexual practices, see Clellan S. Ford and Frank A. Beach, *Patterns of Sexual Behavior* (1951; rpt., New York: Ace Books, n.d.). There is controversy over the relationship between innate drives and culture, but the most sensible position seems to me to have been expressed by Nathan G. Hale, Jr., *Freud and the Americans: The Beginning of Psychoanalysis in the United States, 1876–1917* (New York: Oxford University Press, 1971), pp. 478–79, when he said that "it seems quite certain that historical culture in fact determines the ways in which drives are expressed or, rather, the ways in which society channels this expression."

7 The most convenient sources for American population figures are: J. Potter, "The Growth of Population in America, 1700–1860," in *Population in History: Essays in Historical Demography,* ed. D. V. Glass and D. E. C. Eversley (London: E. Arnold, 1965), pp. 633–88; and Ansley J. Coale and Melvin Zelnik, *New Estimates of Fertility and Population in the United States: A Study of Annual White Births from 1855 to 1960 and of Completeness of Enumeration in Censuses from 1880 to 1960* (Princeton: Princeton University Press, 1963), pp. 36–41.

8 Norman E. Himes' *Medical History of Contraception* (1936); rpt., New York: Shocken Books, 1970) is the ideal starting point for any assessment of birth control. A connection between advocacy of birth control and advocacy of sexual freedom may well make more sense in the twentieth century; I am only speaking of the pre-Margaret Sanger era.

9 A topic treated in detail in Chapter II. Norman Dain, *Concepts of Insanity in the United States, 1789–1865* (New Brunswick, N.J.: Rutgers University Press, 1964), p. 91, begins by asserting that "the role of sex in producing mental illness was given little attention" before the introduction of Freudian theory late in the nineteenth century. Yet on the same page he notes that "the hidden 'vice' of masturbation was most frequently singled out as an important cause of insanity." Joseph F. Kett, "Adolescence and Youth in Nineteenth-Century America," *The Journal of Interdisciplinary History,* II (Autumn 1971), 287, feels that concern for masturbation was part of the process from which emerged a sense of adolescence as a distinct stage of human development.

10 THOMAS WENTWORTH HIGGINSON, "Gymnastics," *Out-Door Papers* (Boston: Ticknor and Fields, 1863), p. 139.

11 There is more on Lewis's respectability in footnote 22 below.

12 LEON HARRIS, *Only to God: The Extraordinary Life of Godfrey Lowell Cabot* (New York: Atheneum, 1967), pp. 168–70, 228–30, 323.

13 PETER T. COMINOS' "Late-Victorian Sexual Respectability and the Social System," *International Review of Social History,* VIII (1963), 18–48, 216–50, is an important, densely written attempt to relate British sexual standards to economic behavior. STEPHEN NISSENBAUM has challenged the connection between restrictive sexual morality and middle-class aspirations in "Sex, Reform, and Social Change" (unpublished paper, delivered at the annual meeting of the Organization of American Historians, April 6, 1972). Nissenbaum does not dispute that the connection might be made later in the century.

14 HALE, *Freud and the Americans,* pp. 466, 465. NISSENBAUM, in "Sex, Reform, and Social Change," argues—I think correctly—that the new sexual consciousness may have had a therapeutic value when it took hold in the 1830s, giving men and women an explanation and a set of cures for the frightening world they found themselves in.

15 SYLVESTER GRAHAM, *Lectures on the Science of Human Life* (London: William Horsell, n.d.), p. vi.

16 EDWARD SHORTER in, "Illegitimacy, Sexual Revolution, and Social Change in Modern Europe," *The Journal of Interdisciplinary History,* II (Autumn 1971), 237–72, portrays a "revolution" in sexual values precisely opposite from the kind of change I see in America: Shorter argues that the advance of capitalism in nineteenth-century Europe brought greater freedom in sexual expressiveness.

17 After arriving at this conclusion some time ago, I discovered that Stephen Nissenbaum has done a good deal more work on the subject; and he, much earlier than I, decided that the 1830s marked a turning point. The 1830s are bound to seem particularly dramatic because innovations in printing markedly increased the volume of material on all subjects. But it still seems that the relative volume of advice literature increased in the 1830s and that its intensity became more shrill. JOHN DEMOS, in "Families in Colonial Bristol, Rhode Island: An Exercise in Historical Demography," *William and Mary Quarterly,* 3d ser., XXV (January 1968), 40–57, suggests that a more liberal sexual morality existed at the end of the eighteenth century.

18 COMINOS, "Late-Victorian Sexual Respectability," pp. 46–47; and CAROL FLORA BROOKS, "The Early History of the Anti-Contraceptive Laws in Massachusetts and Connecticut," *American Quarterly,* XVIII (Spring 1966), 3–23, both give detail on tightening laws in the late nineteenth century.

19 HALE, *Freud and the Americans,* p. 456. *My Secret Life,* abridged (New York: Grove Press, 1966)—the great example of English erotic autobiography (if genuine)—contains instances of servants and poor people who are fully aware of what orthodox morality requires, although they do not always live up to those standards.

[20] There is valuable information on the authors of advice manuals in Michael Gordon and M. Charles Bernstein, "Mate Choice and Domestic Life in the Nineteenth-Century Marriage Manual," *Journal of Marriage and Family,* XXXII (November 1970), 665–74.

[21] Richard Shryock argued that on balance health reform did more good than harm and that some of its principles passed into modern medicine. Shryock, "Sylvester Graham and the Health Reform Movement, 1830–1870," *Mississippi Valley Historical Review,* XVIII (September 1931), 172–83.

[22] Edward Mussey Hartwell, *Physical Training in American Colleges and Universities,* Circulars of Information of the Bureau of Education (Washington: Government Printing Office, 1886), pp. 26–29. Tyler's testimonial to Lewis, along with others of equal enthusiasm, appears in Dio Lewis, *In a Nutshell: Suggestions to American College Students* (New York: Clarke Brothers, 1883), p. 197. Lewis himself did have professional training, including a brief stay at Harvard Medical School, but he had no degree except for an honorary one given him by a homeopathic college in Ohio.

[23] John S. Haller, Jr., "Concepts of Race Inferiority in Nineteenth-Century Anthropology," *Journal of the History of Medicine and Allied Sciences,* XXV (January 1970), 46. See also John D. Davies, *Phrenology, Fad and Science: A Nineteenth Century American Crusade* (New Haven: Yale University Press, 1955).

[24] On eugenics see Mark H. Haller, *Eugenics: Hereditarian Attitudes in American Thought* (New Brunswick, N.J.: Rutgers University Press, 1963); and Donald K. Pickens, *Eugenics and the Progressives* (Nashville: Vanderbilt University Press, 1968). Haller's work, unfortunately, largely ignores early hereditarian thought of the sort appearing in this collection. Cf. Norman E. Himes, "Eugenics Thought in the American Birth Control Movement 100 Years Ago," *Eugenics,* II (May 1929), 3–8.

[25] Joseph W. Howe, *Excessive Venery, Masturbation, and Continence* (New York: Bermingham & Company, 1883); J., *The Sensuous Woman* (New York: Lyle Stuart, 1969); and Robert Chartham, *The Sensuous Couple* (New York: Ballentine Books, 1971).

[26] I have been particularly impressed by the relationships between William Lloyd Garrison and Helen Benson Garrison, and between Theodore Dwight Weld and Angelina Grimké Weld, where sentiment and affection coexisted with acceptance of Victorian norms. Professor Lewis Perry, of the State University of New York, Buffalo, promises to tell a more complicated story when his biography of Henry C. Wright is completed. Wright authored advice books stressing continence, which he apparently practiced with his wife, but he had urges not comprehended in his own theories.

[27] Harold I. Lief, "Teaching Doctors about Sex," in *An Analysis of Human Sexual Response,* ed. Ruth and Edward Beecher (New York: New American Library, 1966), pp. 275–79; *Journal of the American Medical Association,* CIIIC (July 18, 1966), 146.

CHAPTER ONE

Approaching This Delicate Subject

Publicly given advice on sex and matrimony undoubtedly predates the Ten Commandments, and so do the problems which make this advice necessary. But even eternal difficulties inspire differing answers and each generation finds its own approach to persistent questions like those relating to human erotic activity. The manner in which men and women deal with such sensitive issues is not, however, merely a matter of style: the boldness or caution authors employ, the apologies they make to their public, the evils they see and the solutions they are willing to consider, all reveal a great deal about the times, particularly about what society thinks is permissible and about what it fears is amiss. The place to begin, then, is with the way nineteenth-century writers perceived their task as they steeled themselves and their audience to examine various aspects of mankind's sexual nature.

In 1834 Sylvester Graham, a former clergyman lately converted to proper diet as a key to salvation, delivered a series of lectures on chastity. Because Graham was in favor of sexual restraint—a respectable enough position at the time—and because he addressed young men rather than tender-souled young ladies, there would seem to be little potential controversy in printing his talks. Yet standards of public decency, as well as Graham's conscience, drove him, in his preface, to issue an elaborate disclaimer which sought to justify the idea of education on sexual matters.

I am fully aware of the delicacy and difficulty attending the discussion of the subject of the following Lecture [Chastity], and have seriously and solemnly considered all the objections which can be made against its publication; but I am also aware of the immense importance that young men should be correctly and properly instructed on this subject.[1] He who in any manner endeavours to excite the sensual appetites, and arouse the unchaste passions of youth, is one of the most heinous offenders against the welfare of mankind; and, so far as effects are considered, it is not enough that he who meddles with this matter *means well;* irreparable mischief may be done with the best *intentions.* There is no point of morality of more importance; and none that is intrinsically connected with so much difficulty. Through a fear of contaminating the minds of youth, it has long been considered the wisest measure to keep them in ignorance; and too generally, in order to sustain this measure, the natural inquisitiveness of the young mind has been met by misrepresentation and falsehood, on the part of those who would preserve their purity; while, on the other hand, the basest of human cupidity has eagerly catered to the restless and prying curiosity, which has thus been exceedingly augmented. So that, while parents have been resting securely in the idea of the ignorance and purity of their children, these have been clandestinely drinking in the most corrupt and depraving knowledge from mercenary and polluted hands.

I am fully convinced that mankind have erred in judgment and in practice on this point. Truth, properly inculcated, can never be injurious. The only questions are, When and How? As to the *when,* I am decidedly of the opinion that it should be as early as the young mind can be made to understand the subject accurately; and in regard to the manner or the *how,* I am satisfied that it should at first be as purely scientific as possible. Anatomy and Physiology must become common branches of education, and fundamental principles in all our systems of instruction and government, and all our domestic and social customs, before society reaches its highest good. And this kind of knowledge can never be corrupting in its effects nor tendencies. The more perfectly scientific the young mind becomes in anatomy and physiology, the more strongly is it secured against the undue influences of lewd associations; and it learns to think even of the sexual organs with as little lasciviousness as it does of the stomach and lungs. But all this requires great wisdom and prudence.

Graham noted, partly by way of apology, "When I commenced my public career as a lecturer on the Science of Human Life, it did not, in any degree, enter into my plan to treat on this delicate subject. . . ."

Graham was not the only person convinced that the delicate subject had to be broached, and not the only person uneasy about approaching it. Catharine Beecher (an influential educational reformer) and her more famous sister, Harriet Beecher Stowe, collaborated on a book of "Domestic Science" designed to help American women maintain "Economical, Healthful, Beautiful, and Christian Homes." *Compelled to discuss the mother's responsibility for shaping the rising generation's sexual conduct, Beecher and Stowe clearly regarded mention of erotic impulses as a distasteful chore, thrust upon them and their female readers by unkind biological fate.*

There is no more important duty devolving upon a mother, than the cultivation of habits of modesty and propriety in young children.[2] All indecorous words or deportment should be carefully restrained; and delicacy and reserve studiously cherished. It is a common notion, that it is important to secure these virtues to one sex, more than to the other; and, by a strange inconsistency, the sex most exposed to danger is the one selected as least needing care. Yet a wise mother will be especially careful that her sons are trained to modesty and purity of mind.

Yet few mothers are sufficiently aware of the dreadful penalties which often result from indulged impurity of thought. If children, in *future* life, can be preserved from licentious associates, it is supposed that their safety is secured. But the records of our insane retreats, and the pages of medical writers, teach that even in solitude, and without being aware of the sin or the danger, children may inflict evils on themselves, which not infrequently terminate in disease, delirium, and death.

There is no necessity for explanations on this point any farther than this; that certain parts of the body are not to be touched except for purposes of cleanliness, and that the most dreadful suffering comes from disobeying these commands. So in regard to practices and sins of which a young child will sometimes inquire, the wise parent will say, that this is what children cannot understand, and about which they must not talk or ask questions. And they should be told that it is always a bad sign, when children talk on matters which parents call vulgar and indecent, and that the company of such children should be avoided. Disclosing details of wrong-doing to young and curious children, often leads to the very evils feared. But parents and teachers, in this age of danger, should be well informed and watchful; for it is not unfrequently the case, that servants and school-mates will teach young children practices, which exhaust the nervous system and bring on paralysis, mania, and death [as sexual excess was thought to do].

Even men and women less committed to the moral status quo than Catharine Beecher and Harriet Beecher Stowe seldom found it possible to discourse on sexual matters without some acknowledgment of squeamishness. Such was, for instance, the stance adopted by Robert Dale Owen, a forthright man on most social questions. Owen, a visionary virtually by inheritance, was the son of Scottish reformer Robert Owen and himself became an instrumental figure in a notable communitarian experiment at New Harmony, Indiana. By the time he reached middle age, Owen had mellowed enough to achieve success in politics, serving both as congressman and as a representative in the Indiana legislature, where in the 1850s he pressed for more liberal divorce laws. But in 1830 Owen dared author Moral Physiology; Or, A Brief and Plain Treatise on the Population Question, *the first work advocating birth control to be published in America. Although accustomed to controversy and firmly convinced of his rectitude, Owen nevertheless felt that he could not cope with such a sensitive subject—or with public opinion—until his own moral credentials were in order and until he had rebuked prudery. The result was an apologia resembling Sylvester Graham's and bearing kinship to the circumspection of Beecher and Stowe, despite Owen's view of sex (which was more favorable than Graham's) and despite Owen's attack upon the kind of willful ignorance the Beecher sisters seemed to advocate.*

The subject I intend to discuss [birth control] is strictly physiological, although connected, like many other physiological subjects, with political economy, morals, and social science.[3] In discussing it, I must speak as plainly as physicians and physiologists do. What I mean, I must say. Pseudo-civilized man, that anomalous creature who has been not inaptly defined "an animal ashamed of its own body," may take it ill that I speak simply: I cannot help that. . . .

If you have travelled and observed much, you will already have learned the distinction between real and artificial propriety. If you have been in Constantinople, you probably know, that when any one of the grand seignor's wives is ill, the physician is only allowed to see her wrist, which is thrust through an opening in the side of the room, because it is improper even for a physician to look upon another man's wife; and it is thought better to sacrifice health than propriety.

Owen proceeded to give other examples of standards of modesty differing from nineteenth-century America's.

If my reader has seen all or any of these countries and customs, I doubt not that he or she will read my little book understandingly, and interpret it in the purity which springs from enlarged and enlightened views; or, indeed, from common sense. If not—if you who now peruse these lines have been educated at home, and have never passed the boundary line of your own nation—perhaps of your own village—if you have not learned that there are other proprieties besides those of your country; and that, after all, genuine modesty has its legitimate seat in the heart rather than in the outward form or sanctioned custom—then, I fear me, you may chance to cast these pages from you . . . unconscious that the indelicacy lies, not in my simple words . . . but in the pruriently sensitive imagination that discovers impropriety in [them]. . . .

Reader! if you belong to the class of prudes or libertines, I pray you follow my argument no farther. My heresies will not suit you. As a prude you will find them too honest; as a libertine, too temperate. In the former case you will call me a very shocking person; in the latter, a quiz or a bore.

But if you be honest, upright, pure-minded; if you be unconscious of unworthy motives or selfish passion; if truth be your ambition, and the welfare of our race your object—then approach with me a subject most important to man's well-being; and approach it, as I do, in a spirit of dispassionate, disinterested, free inquiry. Approach it, resolving to prove all things, and hold fast that which is good. . . .

Neither is it any concern of yours what my character is, or has been. No man of sense or modesty unnecessarily obtrudes personalities that regard himself on the public. And, most assuredly, it is neither to gratify your curiosity or my vanity, that I now do violence to my feelings, and speak a few words touching myself. I do so, to disarm, if I can, prejudice of her sting; to obtain the ears of the prejudiced; and to acquaint my readers, that they are conversing with one whom circumstance and education have happily preserved from habits of excess and associations of profligacy.

All those who have intimately known the life and private habits of the writer of this little treatise, will bear him witness, that what he now states is true, to the letter. He was indebted to his parents for habits of the strictest temperance—some would call it abstemiousness—in *all* things. He never, at any time, habitually, used ardent spirits, wine, or strong drink of any kind: latterly, he has not even used animal food. He never entered a brothel in his life; nor associated, even for an evening, with those poor, unhappy victims, whom the brutal, yet tolerated vices of man, and their own unsuspicious or ungoverned feelings, betray to misery and degradation. He never sought the company but of the intellectual and self-respecting of the other sex, and has no associations connected with the name of woman, but those of esteem and respectful affection. To this day, he is even girlishly sensitive to the coarse and ribald jests in which young men think it witty to indulge, at the expense of a sex they cannot appreciate. The confidence with which women may have honoured him, he has never selfishly abused; and at this moment, he has not a single wrong with which to reproach himself towards a sex which he considers the equal of man in all the essentials of character, and his superior in generous disinterestedness and moral worth.

We have probably passed the day when "abstemiousness—in *all* things" *qualifies a person as an authority on sex, but Owen's spotless private life presumably established his credibility in 1830. Despite his sincere denials, there was potentially subversive evidence in his argument: documentation of the fact that morals vary from society to society, that propriety in one country may well be impropriety in another. Ever-increasing knowledge of other cultures and of history eventually would play a part in undermining the nineteenth-century conviction that sexual morality was absolute, rigorous, and unchanging. Such doubts, however, were at best vague discontents and stray thoughts when Owen wrote—they only became prevalent at the century's end and in the early years of the twentieth century. Until then, a man like Owen could cling to the orthodox sexual code; and yet at the same time he could exhibit some of the dissatisfaction and engage in some of the questioning which, in succeeding decades, would cast a lengthening shadow across the old morality.*

With misplaced smugness, we might assume that nineteenth-century official sexual morality was so repressive it depended on a conspiracy of silence for its survival—the appeal to fear and to higher authority Catharine Beecher and Harriet Beecher Stowe seemed to be advising American mothers to use on their children. Yet the very works which conveyed sexual orthodoxy frequently railed against common ignorance on erotic subjects and attacked "false modesty" that might prohibit talking about sex. The Beecher family itself was not of one mind on the impropriety of dealing openly with erotic questions. Henry Ward Beecher, brother of Catharine and Harriet, devoted emphatic passages in his Twelve Lectures to Young Men *to an assault upon excessive delicacy regarding sexual matters. One of the most popular ministers of his day, Beecher was a versatile man, providing the public both with tracts on rectitude and with glimpses of its opposite: in 1874 and 1875 he was the principal figure in a well-publicized trial involving his al-*

leged adultery with a parishioner. In his Lectures, *Beecher demonstrated that it was possible to stand forthrightly both for chastity (keystone of orthodox sexual morality) and for greater frankness in discussions of sex.*

So inveterate is the prejudice against introducing into the pulpit the subject of licentiousness, that ministers of the gospel, knowing the vice to be singularly dangerous and frequent, have yet by silence almost complete, or broken only by circuitous allusions, manifested their submission to the popular taste.[4] That vice upon which it has pleased God to be more explicit and full than upon any other; against which he uttered his voice upon Sinai, *Thou shalt not commit adultery* . . . this subject, upon which the Bible does not so much speak as thunder, not by a single bolt, but peal after peal, we are solemnly warned not to introduce into the pulpit! . . .

One difficulty arises from the sensitiveness of unaffected purity. A mind retaining all the dew and freshness of innocence shrinks from the very *idea* of impurity, as if it were a sin to have thought or heard of it, as if even the shadow of the evil would leave some soil upon the unsullied whiteness of the virgin-mind. . . . To any such, who have half wished that I might not speak, I say: Nor would I, did I not know that purity will suffer more by the silence of shame than by the honest voice of truth.

Another difficulty springs from the nature of the English language, which has hardly been framed in a school where it may wind and fit itself to all the phases of impurity. But were I speaking French—the dialect of refined sensualism and of licentious literature, the language of a land where taste and learning and art wait upon the altars of impurity—then I might copiously speak of this evil, nor use one plain word. But I thank God the honest English tongue which I have learned has never been so bred to this vile subservience of evil. . . . We must speak plainly and properly; or else speak by innuendo, which is the Devil's language.

Another difficulty lies in the confused echoes which vile men create in every community when the pulpit disturbs them. Do I not know the arts of cunning men? . . . Men will not quietly be exposed. They foresee the rising of a virtuously retributive public sentiment. . . . Men protest against the indecency of the pulpit, because the pulpit makes them feel their own indecency; they would drive us from the investigation of vice, that they may keep the field open for their own occupancy. . . .

Another difficulty exists in the criminal fastidiousness of the community upon this subject. This is the counterfeit of delicacy. It resembles it less than paste jewels do the pure pearl. Where delicacy, the atmosphere of a pure heart, is lost, or never was had, a substitute is sought; and is found in *forms* of delicacy, not in its *feelings*. It is a delicacy of exterior, of etiquette, of show, of rules; not of *thought,* not of pure *imagination,* not of the crystal-current of the *heart*. . . .

False modesty always judges by the outside; it cares *how* you speak more than *what*. That which would outrage in plain words may be implied furtively, in the sallies of wit or fancy, and be admissible. Every day I see this giggling modesty, which blushes at *language* more than at its *meaning;* which smiles upon base things, if they will appear in the *garb* of virtue. . . . Those who speak plainly what they mean, when they speak at all, are called rude and vulgar; while those upon whose exquisite sentences the dew of indelicacy rests like so many brilliant pearls of the morning upon flowers, are called our moral authors!

Beecher's attempt to distinguish between "false modesty" and the genuine article was basic to nineteenth-century advice literature. Also basic was his concern about public ignorance. Only an urgent need for knowledge and counsel could have justified the flood of writings on sexual ethics and sexual problems. Well realizing this, authors of advice manuals commonly began their treatises with pleas for better, more "scientific" teachings on erotic matters. In many instances what came after the plea would hardly pass as scientific by present-day standards. Numerous authors, for example, urged phrenology as proper discipline to help select a mate and to detect unsavory impulses—phrenology supposedly allowed its practitioners to read an individual's character from the shape of his or her skull. But pseudo-scientist, proto-scientist, scientist, and non-scientist all joined in a chorus telling the public that sex and matrimony were matters for discussion and rational analysis. Dr. Joseph W. Howe, one-time professor of Clinical Surgery at the Bellevue Hospital Medical College, stated the case bluntly, illustrating it with appropriate episodes drawn from his own practice.

A knowledge of the sexual functions or of sexual hygiene is rarely considered to be a necessary part of our early education, and the value of such knowledge as promoting a healthy physical and mental condition is almost entirely overlooked.[5] The age of puberty generally has passed, before the subject is introduced to the youthful mind even in the most casual way. Indeed there is scarcely a subject more completely ignored, although so much of the health and happiness of the race depends on it. The physician whose professional duties bring him a clearer insight into the private lives of his patients, beyond the point where ordinary vision reaches, is about the only one who fully realizes the great necessity for the diffusion of such knowledge, and an education that will prevent those ignorant assaults on the genital organs which in time stunt the vital forces, and whether cured or not, leave their impress on the vital forces of the patients themselves, as well as on their unfortunate offspring. Outside of the profession there are very few who ever get beneath the thin veneering to the rotten wood below, and thus see the difference between the fictitious side of life, and the real or true life of suffering occasioned by ignorance and bad habits, which might easily be avoided by a little care and wholesome advice given by parents, guardians or teachers, or perhaps best of all by the family physician, for he really is the person fitted by his position to give the necessary information in the way or manner that will carry with it its full weight of conviction, and compel a sensible enforcement of the laws which regulate sexual functions, and he can also briefly explain such points in the anatomy and physiology of the organs under consideration, as will facilitate the patient's efforts to do what is expected of him in an intelligent manner. But unfortunately, as things are, at the present day, the damage is usually done before there is a full realization of the means for preventing it. So dense, indeed, is the general ignorance on this important subject that it is not an uncommon event for men and women to enter the married state without any preliminary knowledge whatever, either theoretical or practical, of the sexual relation. It is not long since that an educated man, a patient, told me that when married at the age of twenty-five he was totally unaware of the nature of the sexual relation so far as his part of it was concerned. His wife unfortunately shared the same ignorance. After a few days or rather nights spent in the midst of curious sensations and doubts and fears they obtained the information in some indirect way that the male organ should be introduced into the "water passage" of the female. The gentleman essayed the experiment on several different occasions without success, and was then compelled to the ludicrous necessity of searching for the place with a candle. Even then it was some days before he succeeded in effecting a natural intercourse, and that too after other consultations with friends who were more versed in the matter than they were. This ignorance, of course is more generally confined to women than to men, but there are enough instances among the latter, to make it a matter of surprise even to a physician who ought to be accustomed to surprises.

In Howe's mind enlightenment was not intended as a spur to indulgence, and the instructional techniques he recommended blended the insights of contemporary medical science with quite positive sanctions.

The education of the youthful mind in [sexual] matters need not be thoughtlessly commenced, or hastily terminated. A gradual and systematic formation of correct ideas and habits, should be fostered as the growth of the boy or girl progresses. . . . If the pupil has exhibited signs of unusual sexual precocity, it would be well to point out the results of all unhealthy familiarity with the genitals before discoursing upon their uses in the accomplishment of a most beneficent plan of nature, to imbue the mind with that laudable sense of fear which should invariably accompany any infringement of the law. Fear is an essential element in controlling this class, which has many, very many members. . . .

With that other and much smaller class, who inherit healthy minds, as well as healthy bodies, with little or no disfigurement from exuberant natural passions, it is always safe to add to their general knowledge of anatomy and physiology some additional and special facts relating to the genito-urinary functions. The subject can be approached gradually, suiting the amount of information to the age of the child, and the general development of the perceptive faculties. The command to keep the hands away from the organs, if aided by the watchfulness of a faithful nurse, or mother, will generally succeed in enforcing this sanitary edict. At the same time it is well to see that all sources of temptation to examine themselves should be removed. . . . Fear of evil consequences is without doubt a great moral power in this world, and although it may not be the noblest propelling force, it cannot be dispensed with in the cases under consideration. We are all sadly human. Emerson, with a degree of truth, says that "there is a crack in everything that God has made," and this undoubted fact is true specially of poor human nature. We have not yet reached perfection and probably never will, and we must recognize the value of such a low moral force as fear in the enforcement of sanitary conditions in all matters relating to the sexual or genito-urinary organs.

Howe's candid use of fear as the ultimate support for science and morality would find little sympathy among present-day sex educators, who generally trust reason and choice farther than he did. Howe's assertions, as a modern critic would quickly note, also passed over a very real difficulty—would people raised with the kind of fears he advocated really be informed about sex or would they simply have gained in embarrassment what little they lost in ignorance?

❧ ❧

Whatever the personal fate of men and women brought up according to Howe's prescriptions, fear and shame about sex created considerable problems for Howe's fellow physicians when they approached patients suffering sexual disorders. As the medical profession improved both its status and its standards throughout the nineteenth century, doctors had to weigh their ethical responsibility to heal illness against the dictates of prevailing morality, which implied that sexual functions were too delicate to be discussed between men and women. In a mid-century series of lectures to Pennsylvania medical students Dr. Charles D. Meigs, a noted gynecological authority, depicted some of the consequent tensions when male practitioners treated female maladies.

The relations between the sexes are of so delicate a character, that the duties of a medical practitioner are necessarily more difficult, when he comes to take charge of a patient laboring under any one of the great host of female complaints, than where he is called upon to treat those more general disorders . . . to which the gentler, like the ruder sex is liable.[6] So great, indeed, is the embarrassment arising from fastidiousness on the part either of the female herself, or of the practitioner, or both, that, I am persuaded, much of the ill success of treatment may be justly charged thereto.

EMBARRASSMENTS OF PRACTICE. It is to be observed that a very current opinion exists as to the difficulty of effectually curing many of the diseases of women; and it is as mortifying as it is true, that we do often see the cases of these disorders going the whole round of the profession in any village, town, or city, and falling, at last, into the hands of the quack; either ending in some surprising cure, or leading the victim, by gradual lapses of health and strength, down to the grave, the last refuge of the incurable, or rather the uncured: I say uncured, for it is a clear and well-known truth, that many of these cases are, in their beginning, of light or trifling importance. . . .

All these evils of medical practice spring not, in the main, from any want of competency either in medicines or in medical men, but from the delicacy of the relations existing between the sexes, of which I spoke; and, in a good degree also from want of information among the population in general, as to the import, meaning, and tendency of disorders, manifested by certain trains of symptoms.

It is, perhaps, best, upon the whole, that this great degree of modesty should exist, even though it go to the extent of putting a bar to special researches, without which no very clear and understandable notions can be obtained of the sexual disorders.

I confess I am proud to say, that, in this country generally, and particularly in some parts of it, women prefer to suffer the extremity of danger and pain rather than waive those scruples of delicacy which prevent their maladies from being fully explored. I think this is an evidence of the presence of a fine morality in our society; but nevertheless, it is true that a greater candor on the part of the patient, and a more resolute and careful inquiry on that of the practitioner, would scarcely fail to bring to light, in their early stages, the curable maladies, which, by faults on both sides, are now misunderstood, because concealed and, consequently, mismanaged, and so, rendered at last incurable.

A less self-confident man than Charles Meigs might find moral ambivalence in an ethical code valuing modesty more than individual well-being; but with his combination of priggishness and professionalism, Meigs drew together significant strands in nineteenth-century approaches to the delicate topic of sexuality. He captured the mixture of caution and boldness with which men and women confronted man's erotic nature, treating it with circumspection (to the point of "false modesty") while urging the public to be better informed. The mere fact that doctors like Meigs produced works dealing with sex marked yet another important feature of respectable nineteenth-century literature: sexuality was something more than the moral issue it always had been—it was now a subject for medicine and physiology. Clergymen, although still prominent among authorities on sexual matters, were yielding a place to laymen and especially to physicians, who increasingly defined marriage and erotic activity as requiring scientific knowledge. Of course, Meigs and his contemporaries assumed, with unjustified certainty, that genuine science would only confirm orthodox morality, that rational inquiry and contemporary ethics would reinforce each other. And yet, prudish and mistaken though nineteenth-century advisers often were, they nevertheless set off on lines of investigation which led (after some wide detours) down to the present day. Naturally enough, Meigs, Joseph Howe, the various Beechers, Robert Owen, Sylvester Graham, and most other nineteenth-century writers of advice literature would deny paternity of the modern movement for sex education; and they would be utterly mortified to think they had begun a tradition which resulted in books about anything sensuous. But, for all their fastidiousness and their obsessive moralizing, such nineteenth-century authors pushed along the process, quite unthinkingly, of separating sexual behavior from theology. They commonly set greater sexual enlightenment as a desirable social goal, little suspecting how much more broadly their descendants would define enlightenment.

1 Dr. Sylvester Graham, *Chastity, In a Course of Lectures to Young Men; Intended Also, for the Serious Consideration of Parents and Guardians* (New York: Fowler and Wells, n.d.), i–ii.

[2] Catharine E. Beecher and Harriet Beecher Stowe, *The American Woman's Home: Or, Principles of Domestic Science; Being a Guide to the Formation and Maintenance of Economical, Healthful, Beautiful, and Christian Homes* (New York: J. B. Ford and Company, 1869), pp. 285–86.

[3] Robert Dale Owen, *Moral Physiology; Or, A Brief and Plain Treatise on the Population Question* (London: J. Watson, 1841), pp. 5–9.

[4] Henry Ward Beecher, *Twelve Lectures to Young Men, On Various Important Subjects,* rev. ed. (New York: D. Appleton and Company, 1879), pp. 124–28. Beecher published various revisions of his lectures throughout his career, the first appearing in 1844. Presumably the passages quoted gained in meaning, coming after Beecher's involvement in scandal and his aquittal on charge of adultery (by courts, if not public opinion).

[5] Joseph W. Howe, M.D., *Excessive Venery, Masturbation and Continence. The Etiology, Pathology and Treatment of the Diseases Resulting from Venereal Excesses, Masturbation and Continence* (New York: Bermingham & Company, 1883), pp. 17–19, 20–22.

[6] Charles D. Meigs, M.D., *Woman: Her Diseases and Remedies. A Series of Letters to His Class,* 4th ed. (Philadelphia: Blanchard and Lea, 1859), pp. 34–35.

CHAPTER TWO

A Destructive Impulse

Twentieth-century advice manuals usually regard sex as natural and (within proper boundaries) as good. There have been exceptions and it would be possible to compile a collection of antisexual diatribes from the last seventy years. Yet even these would most likely sound positively cheerful compared to the dire warnings about erotic activity appearing time after time in nineteenth-century publications. Although individual self-fulfillment is the predominant goal of present-day sexual lore, preservation from supposed moral, mental, and physical destruction was the frequent objective of nineteenth-century writers, who thought of sex as a powerful and disturbing force in life, needing the firmest of controls placed upon it.

Books and pamphlets portraying the terrible effects of sexual indulgence became especially common and especially strident after 1830, perhaps because by then economic change, growth of urban centers, and breakdown of older forms of social control all seemed to jeopardize moral order. Yet writers after 1830 did build upon existing traditions, upon European and American medical treatises dating back into the previous century, which cautioned against erotic excesses. An important example of this earlier literature, Benjamin Rush's Medical Inquiries and Observations, upon the Diseases of the Mind, *serves as a reminder that sexual attitudes cannot be dated with the precision of some historical events. Rush, writing in 1812 (the year of his death), outlined much of what would become far more prevalent twenty years later. Rush was himself relic of times past, a signer of the Declaration of Independence, and a significant figure in the American Revolution as well as in the history of American medicine.*

This [sexual] appetite, which was implanted in our natures for the purpose of propagating our species, when excessive, becomes a disease both of the body and mind.[1] When restrained, it produces tremors, a flushing of the face, sighing, nocturnal pollutions, hysteria, hypochondriasis, and in women the furor uterinus. When indulged in an undue or a promiscuous intercourse with the female sex, or in onanism [masturbation], it produces seminal weakness, impotence, dysury, tabes dorsalis, pulmonary consumption, dyspepsia, dimness of sight, vertigo, epilepsy, hypochondriasis, loss of memory, manalgia, fatuity, and death. . . .

But these are not all the melancholy and disgusting effects of excess in the indulgence of the sexual appetite. They sometimes discover themselves in the imagination and senses, in a fondness for obscene conversation and books, and in a wanton dalliance with women, long after the ability to gratify the appetite has perished from disease, or age.

Having asserted that sexual excess was an illness that produced other illnesses, Rush recommended cures for the dread disease. Because these also foreshadowed post-1830 writings, they will appear in their place later in this collection. Meanwhile, it is task enough to recapture the manifold descriptions post-1830 authorities gave of sex's alleged pathology. In 1879 Elizabeth Blackwell, the first professionally trained American woman physician, made perhaps the most imaginative claim of all. "The growth of pessimism in Germany," *Dr. Blackwell believed,* "is the direct result of increasing licentiousness in a race created with a high ideal of virtue and cherishing a love of home." [2]

❧ ❧

Writers less concerned with German philosophy than Dr. Blackwell found alarming enough consequences to stem from erotic activity. Forty-five years before Dr. Blackwell set pen to paper, Sylvester Graham, with his genius for casting prejudices into scientific terminology, depicted the physiological damage sexuality produced.

The convulsive paroxysms attending venereal indulgence, are connected with the most intense excitement, and cause the most powerful agitation to the whole system that it is ever subject to.[3] The brain, stomach, heart, lungs, liver, skin, and the other organs, feel it sweeping over them with the tremendous violence of a tornado. The powerfully excited and convulsed heart drives the blood, in fearful congestion, to the principal viscera, producing oppression, irritation, debility, rupture, inflammation, and sometimes disorganization; and this violent paroxysm is generally succeeded by great exhaustion, relaxation, lassitude, and even prostration.

These excesses, too frequently repeated, cannot fail to produce the most terrible effects. The nervous system, even to its most minute filamentary extremities, is tortured into a state of debility, and excessive irritability, and uncontrollable mobility, and aching sensibility; and the vital contractility of the muscular tissues throughout the whole system becomes exceedingly impaired, and the muscles generally become relaxed and flaccid; and consequently, all the organs and vessels of the body, even to the smallest capillaries, become extremely debilitated, and their functional powers exceedingly feeble.

Aware that even such strong words might well not convert his youthful male audience to virtual celibacy, Graham further sought to reconcile his hearers to physiology's iron laws.

Let no one demur at this [limitation of intercourse]. Remember, my young friends, the end of your organization! Recollect that the *final cause* of your organs of reproduction—the propagation of your species—requires but seldom the exercise of their function! and remember that the higher capabilities of man qualify him for more exalted and exalting pleasures than lie within the precincts of sensual enjoyment! and remember, also, that by all we go beyond the real wants of nature in the indulgence of our appetites, we debase our intellectual and moral powers, increase the carnal influences over our mental and moral faculties, and circumscribe our field of rational acquisition and ennobling pleasures.

Who, then, would yield to sensuality, and forego the higher dignity of his nature, and be contented to spend his life, and all his energies in the low satisfactions of a brute! when earth and heaven are full of motives for noble and exalting enterprize? and when time and eternity are the fields which lie before him, for his achievements of virtue, happiness, immortality, and unperishable glory?

Graham devoted fifty more pages to promotion of chastity—perhaps indication he was secretly unconvinced that even Jacksonian America offered sufficient enterprises to divert sexual energy satisfactorily.

Few of Graham's contemporaries were more proficient at giving advice than William Andrus Alcott. Better informed than Graham (although largely in agreement with his dietary and hygienic ideas), Alcott was a school-teacher turned physician. A combination of ill health and fortunate opportunities led Alcott to a remarkable literary career—he published voluminously on physiology, education, and moral subjects. Written for laymen, Alcott's books and articles served to transmit medical and educational theories to a large public in pre–Civil War years. Among those theories were to be found grim words for youth, particullarly those drawn by the glitter of America's rapidly expanding cities.

Large cities and thinly settled places are the *extremes* of social life.[4] Here, of course, vice will be found in its worst forms. It is more difficult to say which extreme is worst, among *an equal number of individuals;* but probably the city; for in the country, vice is oftener solitary [masturbation], and less frequently social [prostitution]; while in the city it is not only *social* but also *solitary.*

A well informed gentleman from New Orleans, of whose own virtue by the way, I have not the *highest* confidence, expressed, lately the strongest apprehension that the whole race of young men in our cities, of the present generation, will be ruined. Others have assured me that in the more northern cities, the prospect is little, if any, more favorable. . . .

There is now in Pennsylvania—it seems unnecessary to name the place—a man thirty-five years old, with all the infirmities of "three score and ten." Yet his premature old age, his bending and tottering form, wrinkled face, and hoary head, might be traced to solitary and social *licentiousness.*

This man is not alone. There are thousands in every city who are going the same road; some with slow and cautious steps, others with a fearful rapidity. Thousands of youth on whom high expectations have been placed, are already on the highway that will probably lead down to disease and premature death.

Although opposed to all forms of sexual "excess," Alcott devoted especial attention to masturbation.

The Young ought at least to know, briefly, to what a formidable host of maladies secret vice is exposed.

1. *Insanity.* The records of hospitals show that insanity, from solitary indulgence, is common. . . .

2. *Chorea Sancti Viti,* or *St. Vitus's dance. . . .*

3. *Epilepsy.* Epileptic or *falling sickness fits,* as they are sometimes denominated, are another very common scourge of secret vice. . . .

4. *Idiotism. . . .*

5. *Paralysis* or *Palsy,* is no uncommon punishment of this transgression. . . .

6. *Apoplexy.* This has occasionally happened; though more rarely.

7. *Blindness,* in some of its forms. . . . Indeed a weakness of sight is among the first symptoms that supervene on these occasions.

8. *Hypochrondria.* This is as much a disease by itself as the small pox, though many regard it otherwise. The mind is diseased, and the individual has many imaginary sufferings, it is true; but the imagination would not be thus unnaturally awake, if there were no accompanying disturbance in the bodily functions. Hypochondria, in its more aggravated forms, is a very common result of secret vice.

9. *Phthisis,* or consumption, is still more frequently produced by the cause we are considering, than any other disease I have mentioned. . . . Is it not madness to expose ourselves to its attacks for the shortlived gratifications of a moment?

Alcott was—fortunately for the species—wrong; erotic activity has no such frightening consequences. Feelings of guilt about masturbation are another matter and an admission made by Alcott hints that fear (of the sort Alcott's writings encouraged) produced more damage than excess itself ever could. After giving several examples of lives destroyed, presumably by "secret vice," Alcott noted: "The reader should remember that the persons whose miseries are here described, were generally sufferers from *hypochondria.* They had not advanced to the still more horrid stages of palsy, apoplexy, epilepsy, idiotism, St. Vitus's dance, blindness, or insanity." *It was (to use Alcott's term) their* "imaginary sufferings" *which so tortured them and which, in the process, became tragically real.*

Alcott's emphasis on masturbation was partly a judgment on his audience—young, unmarried men. Much the same sort of emphasis, and much the same kind of mournful predictions, appeared in general advice literature throughout the rest of the nineteenth century. If anything, the list of horrible symptoms grew longer as the decades passed. In 1877, Dr. Harvey Kellogg, delivering Plain Facts About Sexual Life, *compiled a truly awe-inspiring guide to* "Suspicious signs" *parents should look for to detect the* "secret vice" *among their children.*

1. *General debility,* coming upon a previously healthy child . . . when it cannot be traced to any other legitimate cause . . . may safely be attributed to solitary vice, no matter how far above natural suspicion the individual may be. . . .[5]

2. *Early symptoms of consumption.* . . .

3. *Premature and defective development.* . . .

4. *Sudden change in disposition.* . . .

5. *Lassitude* is as unnatural for a child as for a young kitten. . . .

6. In connection with the preceding symptom will generally be found, instead of that natural brilliance of expression in the eyes and countenance, an unnatural dullness and vacantness altogether foreign to childhood. This is a just ground for suspicion.

7. *Sleeplessness* is another symptom of some value. . . .

8. *Failure of mental capacity* without apparent cause should occasion suspicion of evil practices. . . .

9. *Fickleness.* . . .

10. *Untrustworthiness.* . . .

11. *Love of solitude* is a very suspicious sign. . . .

12. *Bashfulness.* . . .

13. *Unnatural boldness.* . . .

14. *Mock piety.* . . .

15. *Easily frightened.* . . .

16. *Confusion of ideas* is another characteristic of the devotee of this awful vice. . . .

17. Boys in whom the habit has become well developed sometimes manifest a decided aversion to the society of girls; but this is not nearly so often the case as some authors seem to indicate. It would rather appear that the opposite is more often true. Girls usually show an increasing fondness for the society of boys, and are very prone to exhibit marked evidence of real wantonness.

18. *Round shoulders* and a stooping posture in sitting are characteristics of young masturbators of both sexes. . . .

19. *Weak backs and pains in the limbs and stiffness of the joints* in children are familiar signs of the habit. . . .

20. *Paralysis* of the lower extremities, coming on without apparent cause, is not infrequently the result of solitary indulgence, even in very small children. . . .

21. The *gait* of a person addicted to this vice will usually betray him to one who has learned to distinguish the peculiarities which almost always mark the walk of such persons. . . .

22. *Bad positions* in bed are evidences which should be noticed. If a child lies constantly upon its abdomen, or is often found with its hands about the genitals, it may be at least considered in a fair way to acquire the habit if it has not already done so.

23. *Lack of development of the breasts* in females, after puberty, is a common result of self-pollution. . . .

24. *Capricious appetite*. . . .

25. One very constant peculiarity of such children is their extreme fondness for unnatural, hurtful, and irritating articles. Nearly all are greatly attached to salt, pepper, spices, cinnamon, cloves, vinegar, mustard, horse-radish, and similar articles, and use them in most inordinate quantities. . . .

26. *Eating clay, slate pencils, plaster, chalk,* and other indigestible articles is a practice to which girls who abuse themselves are especially addicted. . . .

27. Disgust for simple food. . . .

28. *The use of tobacco* is good presumptive evidence that a boy is also addicted to a practice still more filthy. . . .

29. *Unnatural paleness* and colorless lips, unless they can be otherwise accounted for. . . .

30. *Acne, or pimples,* on the face are also among the suspicious signs, especially when they appear upon the forehead as well as upon other portions of the face. . . .

31. *Biting the finger nails* is a practice very common in girls addicted to this vice. . . .

32. The eyes often betray much. . . .

33. An habitually moist, cold hand. . . .

34. Palpitation of the heart, frequently occurring, denotes a condition of nervous disturbance which has some powerful cause, and which may often be found to be the vice in question.

35. *Hysteria* in females may be regarded as a suspicious circumstance when frequently occurring on very slight occasions, and especially if there is no hereditary tendency to the disease.

36. *Chlorosis,* or *green sickness.*

37. *Epileptic fits* in children are not infrequently the result of vicious habits.

38. *Wetting the bed.* . . .

39. *Unchastity of speech* and fondness for obscene stories betray a condition of mind which does not exist in youth who are not addicted to this vice.

Because these "suspicious signs" *were not conclusive, Dr. Kellogg also gave* "positive signs," *the most positive of which was:*

1. Detection in the act.

Dr. Kellogg devoted another thirty-one somewhat technical pages to other dreadful ailments that he believed followed upon habitual "self-pollution."

Kellogg and Sylvester Graham were extreme in their hostility to erotic indulgence, but masturbation seemed a heinous sin even to people who, on some sexual issues, might be counted as positively radical by nineteenth-century standards. Marx Edgeworth Lazarus was one such person; he was a wealthy homeopathic doctor who, influenced by European utopian thought, argued in 1852 that conventional marriage was unduly restrictive and that a wider margin of "passional liberty" *would produce greater happiness. Another work, published the same year, made it plain that Lazarus' radicalism did not comprehend* "self-abuse." *Lazarus equalled Kellogg and Graham in the disgust he held for masturbation, in part because he valued heterosexual activity more than they did; autoeroticism ran counter to his reformist (and idealistic) conception of relationships between the sexes.*

Masturbation, which is merely the ultimate expression of a morbid state of spiritual introversion, is the futile attempt of indolence to cheat the intentions of nature, and by a simply subjective act of the imagination, aided by the genital organs, to enjoy the pleasures of love without earning, without conquering them, without the energetic exercise of those virtues of soul and body which win woman's favor: so conversely, of woman in respect to man.[6]

As it is impossible to conceive an act, which, if committed with impunity, would more effectually defeat the ends of human existence, removing at once the most powerful incentives to individual development and the sweetest accords of social harmony; so we are not surprised to find it visited with condign punishment, to find its subject and victim reduced to such wretchedness as causes other sufferings to appear to him enviable; an unutterable horror to himself, an object of scorn to society, and of whom, in his impotence and corruption, it would be difficult to say whether it is rather a soul that drags along a corpse, or a moving body, whose soul is extinct; were it not that amid the wreck of all other faculties, consciousness is only intensified and prolonged through the hours when other beings sleep, in order that the punishment may be complete, and that no particle of anguish may be lost. Idiotcy [sic.] or madness sometimes close the record.

Lazarus did see cause for national pride in this otherwise grim picture:

Fortunately, in the United States, the necessities of a livelihood and the absence of encouragement to idle luxury leave comparatively few permanent victims to such habits of introversion [as stimulate men and women to practice masturbation].

Clearly, the appalling results of "secret vice" *possessed a special interest for advice-manual authors, attracting their attention in almost embarrassing detail. There is an obvious explanation available: perhaps masturbation was more common than any other form of sexual indulgence. Although authors presumably would have no accurate way of knowing this, changes in nineteenth-century society may well have led them to believe it to be true. The isolation experienced by new arrivals to urban areas, simultaneous production of larger homes and smaller families, the growth of boarding schools, increasing removal of middle-class children from the workday world of adults—all these developments either presented more opportunities for solitary indulgence or made it more plausible for parents to worry that their children had the privacy autoerotic activity demands. Such developments, which were well underway by 1830, do go a step toward indicating why nineteenth-century literature took masturbation more seriously than did eighteenth-century publications.*

There are other possible interpretations of nineteenth-century fascination with "secret vice." *Some appeal may have been in the act's secrecy. Americans (particularly in the antebellum period) were proficient at detecting clandestine activity of all sorts: alleged plots by Masons, Catholics, and Mormons, slave-power conspiracies and anti-slave-power conspiracies. Hidden depravity was merely an additional concealed evil, another sinister assault on the moral order. A similarly tempting—and likewise virtually unprovable—explanation is far more psychological than social, drawing upon the fact that the authorities continually harped on masturbation's supposedly self-destructive nature: it was "self-*abuse*" and "self-*pollution." *There could scarcely be a more straightforward way of representing sex as a personal impulse with which each human being (including authors of advice manuals, presumably) must struggle. Concern for masturbation, then, easily became a screen upon which to project one's own unconscious battle with drives that orthodox morality demanded be subjugated.*

Whatever their psychological or social origins, nineteenth-century descriptions of autoeroticism had an importance transcending their general inaccuracy, especially because they focused on youth at a time when so many contemporary ideas about childhood were being formed. Crudely developed as cautionary writings were, they marked a vague awareness of infantile sexuality, a subject Sigmund Freud would dissect far more skillfully and significantly at the century's end. Although much American prose of the day fastened upon childish innocence (as advice literature often did), hidden in odd paragraphs and stray lines were cases of very young children, even infants, whose sexual nature was dreadfully revealed to the author. Nineteenth-century writers also fashioned the concept of adolescence, an idea we take for granted although it is actually of comparatively recent origin (previous generations simply expected youth to assume adult duties at a far younger age than at present). Cautionary literature, with its continual fretting about resisting sexual activity in the decade or more between puberty and marriage, encouraged people to regard these years as a special time with special problems (including sexual ones), much as we now regard adolescence. Finally, anti-masturbatory writings called attention to another feature of emerging consciousness about childhood: acknowledgment of the peer group's importance. Time after time, authors warned mothers and fathers that children could be corrupted by other children, tacitly conceding that authority and knowledge no longer flowed downward from parents but rather that, with increasing privacy at home and with large parts of days spent in schools, children were gaining their own sources of information and status, ones beyond parents' control.

The personal effects of cautionary literature cannot be measured with any accuracy; there are too few direct indications whether men and women exposed to preachings against self-indulgence walked purity's straight and narrow path or grew up with an oppressive weight of fear and guilt for their youthful lapses. But there were obvious human consequences to the manner in which authorities perceived masturbation, and the vigor with which they searched out "signs" *of it. Needless shame and suffering, as well as inattention to real ailments, were the fates of people whose maladies were blandly diagnosed as products of* "self-pollution." *Reports of insane asylums noted, with mistaken statistical precision, souls driven mad (so doctors confidently thought) by their own willful excesses. Authors like Graham and Alcott, properly righteous, reprinted sad statements from penitent masturbators, convinced that their blighted lives were punishment for voluntary erotic transgressions—God's wrath being visited through physiological laws. Those documents convey better than any other source the tragically exacting demands put on men and women when they are made to believe that following deeply implanted urges leads irrevocably to destruc-*

tion. "Were I not restrained by *sentiments of religion," one of Alcott's correspondents (an addict of "self-pollution") told him,* "I should ere this have put an end to my existence; which is the more insupportable as it is caused by myself." [7]

Masturbation, despite its prominence in cautionary literature, was not the only kind of sexual excess thought to be harmful; any sort of frequent indulgence (even within marriage) produced much the same results, according to a large number of authorities. Yet few writers, and probably an even smaller percentage of the general public, had any thought of absolute celibacy. Sexuality was a destructive impulse—but also necessary. And so, despite the seemingly antisexual tone of much advice literature, authors commonly saw themselves as primarily responsible for drawing the boundary between good and bad erotic activity, for finding the proper sphere of something so essential and so potentially dangerous as sex. This involved determining how much continence was desirable—and here there was disagreement.

Some authorities devoted themselves to demonstrating that there was no harm in sexual abstinence. "Is continence physically injurious?" *was the rhetorical question of Dr. Augustus K. Gardner, a medical man of importance. He answered with a firm* "no." *In somewhat tortured prose, he concluded,* "It is determined in our opinion that the commerce of the sexes has no necessities that cannot be restrained without peril, and the very lively solicitations which spring from the genital sense, have no other end than to insure the perpetuity of the race by the attraction of pleasure." [8] *This was Gardner's way of saying that continence was better than sexual activity and that the latter was to be strictly reserved for procreation, not mere enjoyment.*

Dr. Gardner's position did not go unchallenged. Samuel R. Wells, the phrenologist, made a case for some sexual activity in addition to the bare minimum reproduction required. By this, Wells very strictly meant intercourse within matrimony: it took exceptional (and exceptionally bold) people to advocate illicit sexual indulgence. To buttress his argument, Wells drew upon statistical evidence, as advice-book authors were beginning to do in the nineteenth century.

Men and women are celibates in violation of Nature's laws. Every function of body and every faculty of mind was made to be exercised, and the non-exercise of any one of them is always followed by evil effects, involving not only the organ or function immediately concerned, but all the others.[9] The whole system participates in the derangement which supervenes. . . .

Dr. Stark, Registrar-General of Scotland, finds, according to his recently published memoir, that, in that country, the death-rate of the bachelors between the ages of twenty and twenty-five years is double that of the married men. As the age increases the difference between the death-rates of the married and unmarried decreases; but it still shows a marked advantage in favor of the married men at each quinquennial period of life. . . .

Voltaire said: "The more married men you have, the fewer crimes there will be. . . ."

Whatever may be said of Voltaire's theology, his statement on the marriage question is certainly correct. Statistics prove that a large majority of our criminals, State prison convicts, etc., are unmarried. Think of this, young men; and if you wish to escape all that is bad, try to form a partnership with a good woman, and you will be secure.

Dr. Joseph W. Howe was less circumspect than Wells.

The genital organs are not exempted from the general law, viz: that the neglect to fulfill a function may be followed by a loss of power to perform that function in a natural manner.[10] It is true that a man may go for years without intercourse, may then marry, and be able to copulate with success; but such cases are exceptional. The organs of generation were intended for the propagation of the species during adult life, and the performance of their functions in the married state conduces to a healthy condition of mind and body.

Likewise willing to put in a good word for a moderate amount of intercourse was Dr. Charles Knowlton, whose Fruits of Philosophy *(1832) was one of the pioneering American birth control treatises.*

While the gratification of the reproductive instinct in such manner as I have mentioned [masturbation, sexual excess] leads to bad consequences, a temperate and natural gratification, under proper circumstances, is attended with good—besides the mere attendant pleasure, which alone is enough to recommend such gratification.[11] I admit that human beings might be so constituted that if they had no reproductive instinct to gratify, they might enjoy good health; but being constituted as they are, this instinct cannot be mortified with impunity. It is a fact universally admitted, that unmarried females do not enjoy so much good health and attain to so great an age as the married; notwithstanding that the latter are subject to the diseases and pains incident to child-bearing. A temperate gratification promotes the secretions, and the appetite for food; calms the restless passions; induces pleasant sleep; awakens social feeling, and adds a zest to life which makes one conscious that life is worth preserving.

As Howe's and Knowlton's statements imply, it was quite possible both to value sexual activity and to think that too much of it was highly destructive. One of the facts preventing any simple judgment on nineteenth-century advice manuals is the way authors mingled anti-sexual arguments with passages clearly portraying sex (properly restrained) as beneficial, even uplifting. Dr. Elizabeth Blackwell, a harsh critic of licentiousness, captured some of the ambivalence:

Physical passion is not in itself evil; on the contrary, it is an essential part of our nature.[12] It is an endowment which, like every other human faculty, has the power of high growth. It possesses that distinctive human characteristic—receptivity to mental impressions. These impressions blend so completely with itself, as to change its whole character and effect; and it thus becomes an ennobling or a degrading agent in our lives.

Dr. John Harvey Kellogg, no friend to sensuality, resembled Dr. Blackwell in his interpretation of sex's dual nature.

Just in proportion as the perpetuation of the race is more important than the existence of any single individual, the organs of reproduction may be said to rank higher than any other organs of the human frame, since to them is intrusted the important duty of performing that most marvelous of all vital processes, the production of living beings.[13] That this high rank in the vital economy is recognized by nature, is shown by the fact that she has attached to the abuse of the generative function the most terrible penalties which can be inflicted upon a living being. . . .

The *use* of the reproductive function is perhaps the highest physical act of which man is capable; its *abuse* is certainly one of the most grievous outrages against nature which it is possible for him to perpetrate.

Although Drs. Blackwell and Kellogg were capable of enthusiasm about the right kind of sexual activity, a world of difference seems to separate them (and most authors of advice manuals) from the nineteenth-century's small clusters of genuine sex radicals, men and women who defied conventional marital customs and who sought freer erotic ex-

pression. Although sometimes strident, sex radicals were tiny and unpopular voices; but they too deserve to be heard, in part because, if we listen closely—beyond the dissonance between them and more straight-laced authors—we can detect a harmony. In the following passage John Humphrey Noyes, founder of Oneida Community, explains how a form of birth control could accomplish something of a demystification of intercourse. This is a strikingly different way of looking at sex from the fearsome admiration of previous authorities—until Noyes' conclusion.

The separation of the amative from the propagative [by means of contraception], places amative sexual intercourse on the same footing with other ordinary forms of social interchange.[14] So long as the amative and propagative are confounded, sexual intercourse carries with it physical consequences which necessarily take it out of the category of mere social acts. . . . [Since females must bear unwanted children] it is not to be wondered at that women, to a considerable extent, look upon ordinary sexual intercourse with more dread than pleasure, regarding it as a stab at their life, rather than a joyful act of fellowship. But separate the amative from the propagative—let the act of fellowship stand by itself—and sexual intercourse becomes a purely social affair, the same in kind with other modes of kindly communion, differing only by its superior intensity and beauty. . . .

In society trained to these principles, as propagation will become a science, so amative intercourse will have place among the "fine arts." Indeed, it will take rank above music, painting, sculpture, etc.; for it combines the charms and benefits of them all. There is as much room for cultivation of taste and skill in this department as in any.

The practice which we propose will give new speed to the advance of civilization and refinement. The self-control, retention of life, and ascent out of sensualism, which must result from making freedom of love a bounty on the chastening of physical indulgence, will raise the race to new vigor and beauty, moral and physical. And the refining effects of sexual love (which are recognized more or less in the world) will be increased a thousand-fold, when sexual intercourse becomes an honored method of innocent and useful communion, and each is married to all.

Sex as an art form! Few ideas could have been more scandalous under the terms of nineteenth-century official morality. Yet the gap between orthodoxy and sexual radicalism was not absolute. Guardians of restraint, the Blackwells and the Kelloggs, had conceded a sublimity to intercourse, when properly directed; Noyes merely pressed this logic to an extreme conclusion—sex became for him the grandest kind of social interaction. And Noyes thought of "self-control" and "ascent out of sensualism" to be among his program's goals, just as advice-book authors regarded them to be essential to true morality. Nor was Noyes dishonest on this point. In common with other sex reformers, he expected erotic expression, if unencumbered by taboo, to result in a higher sort of chastity than that presently enforced by law and fear. Stephen Pearl Andrews, whose anarchism extended to abolition of traditional matrimony, put the hopes of sex radicals like Noyes and himself succinctly. Andrews believed that increased sexual freedom would "moderate the passions instead of inflaming them, and so . . . contribute, in the highest degree, to a general Purity of life." [15] Conventional marriage, Noyes, Andrews, and their cohorts believed, encouraged sexual depravity; destruction of compulsory permanent monogamous relationships would permit only pure and ennobling intercourse, desired by both parties. Thus the radical vision, no less than the orthodox one, rested on refined notions of purity and a sharp sense of what constituted legitimate sexual activity.

It would, of course, be foolish to deny quite real and significant differences between most authors to advice manuals and the sex radicals (just as it would be foolish to deny differences within each group). Yet men and women in nineteenth-century America operated inside a certain cultural consensus. Almost everyone agreed in a general way that the sexual instinct had to be guided if it were not to be destructive of health and happiness; and almost everyone agreed that sex, deprived of its destructive potential, could become as great a force for good as it was for evil.

Nineteenth-century assessments of erotic drives have little to recommend them by way of scientific accuracy; few people raised under more relaxed and permissive codes would voluntarily exchange their world for one in which sexual misconduct was supposed to bring on the most dire consequences. Yet, despite the suffering orthodox morality undoubtedly caused some men and women, there were aspects of it that command respect. For all its thunderous warnings against excess, it was not necessarily anti-erotic; it may even have placed a greater premium on sexual intercourse (of the proper sort) than most twentieth-century authorities would. To assert, as John Harvey Kellogg did, that "use of the reproductive function is perhaps the highest physical act of which man is capable," puts as much a burden on performance as was placed on nonperformance by Kellogg's own statements in favor of chastity. Furthermore, muddled though nineteenth-century writers were, they nevertheless moved toward a more precise and rational study of erotic *impulses. Their use of statistics was appalling—but it was also the beginning of our faith that empirical work can be done on intimate aspects of human behavior, that mere repetition of religious dogma and of popular prejudices does not provide sufficient information on man's nature. Even phrenologists, those oracles of pseudo-science, played a role leading to modern inquiry. Their books abounded in charts and drawings of human heads, customarily locating the faculty of "amativeness" somewhere at the back of the skull. It seems almost laughable to think that sexual drives might correlate with the width of the neck between the ears—this is not a measurement made by present-day sex researchers. All their solemn folly aside, phrenologists did direct study of sexuality to the human anatomy, rather than resting content with pure speculation and a smattering of theology, as many earlier authorities had. Perhaps the kindest judgments to be made about nineteenth-century analyses of the nature of erotic impulses are that they were neither so simple nor so antisexual as stereotype would have it, and that they began avenues of research which would broaden in time. Nevertheless, a reader who took advice literature to heart faced a trying time resisting sexuality's lures in a society that seemed filled with depraving influences.*

---

1 BENJAMIN RUSH, *Medical Inquiries and Observations, upon the Diseases of the Mind* (Philadelphia: Kimber & Richardson, 1812), pp. 347, 350.

2 DR. ELIZABETH BLACKWELL, *Counsel to Parents on the Moral Education of Their Children* (New York: Brentano's Literary Emporium, 1879), p. 61, fn.

3 DR. SYLVESTER GRAHAM, *Chastity, in a Course of Lectures to Young Men: Intended Also for the Serious Consideration of Parents and Guardians* (New York: Fowler and Wells, n.d.), pp. 5–6, 15.

4 WILLIAM A. ALCOTT, *The Young Man's Guide,* 16th ed. (Boston: T. R. Marvin, 1846), pp. 314–15, 337–40, 344.

5 J. H. KELLOGG, *Plain Facts about Sexual Life* (Battle Creek, Mich.: Office of the Health Reformer, 1877), pp. 249–60, 265.

6 M. EDGEWORTH LAZARUS, *Involuntary Seminal Losses: Their Causes, Effects, and Cure* (New York: Fowlers and Wells, 1852), pp. 45–47.

7 ALCOTT, *Young Man's Guide,* pp. 342–43.

8 AUGUSTUS K. GARDNER, *The Conjugal Relationships as Regards Personal Health and Hereditary Well-Being, Practically Treated,* 5th English ed. (Glasgow: Thomas D. Morison, 1905), pp. 43–44. The date of this edition proves the longevity of such sexual advice: Gardner died in 1879.

9 S. R. WELLS, *Wedlock; Or, the Right Relations of the Sexes: Disclosing the Laws of Conjugal Selection, and Showing Who May, and Who May Not Marry* (New York: Samuel R. Wells, Publisher, 1869), pp. 130–33.

10 JOSEPH W. HOWE, *Excessive Venery, Masturbation, and Continence. The*

Etiology, Pathology, and Treatment of the Diseases Resulting from Venereal Excesses, Masturbation, and Continence (New York: Bermingham & Company, 1883), pp. 184–85.

11 CHARLES KNOWLTON, *Fruits of Philosophy: An Essay on the Population Question,* 2nd new ed. (London: Annie Besant and Charles Bradlaugh, n.d. [1877?]), p. 54.

12 BLACKWELL, *Counsel to Parents,* p. 73.

13 KELLOGG, *Plain Facts,* p. 73.

14 JOHN HUMPHREY NOYES, *Male Continence* (Oneida: N.Y.: Office of the Oneida Circular, 1872), pp. 15–16. Noyes was quoting, approvingly, one of his own earlier works.

15 STEPHEN PEARL ANDREWS, ed., *Love, Marriage, and Divorce, and the Sovereignty of the Individual* (New York: Stringer and Townsend, 1853), p. 20.

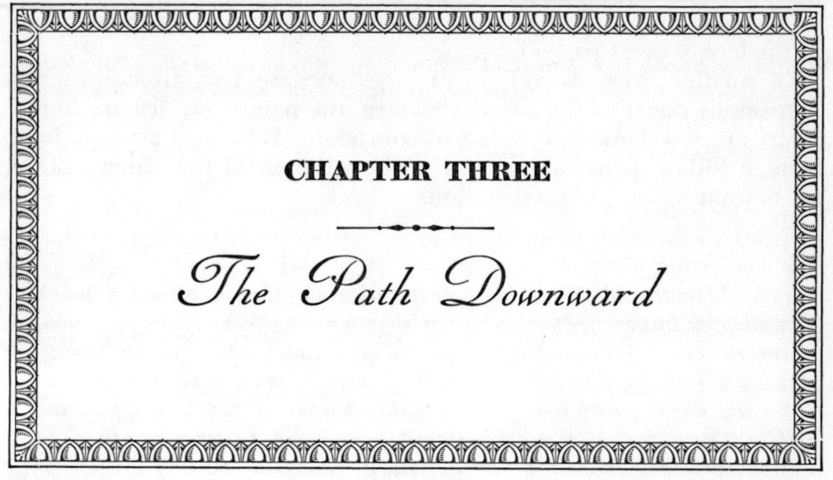

CHAPTER THREE

The Path Downward

Life in nineteenth-century America (as it appeared in advice books) was fraught with moral perils, gaudy temptations luring men and women into sexual excess and eventual destruction. Such dangers were particularly strong in cities, and orthodox morality spoke with special force to Americans attempting to cope with urbanization, inspiring them to practice self-control as they became cut off from traditional restraints operative in small towns, settled communities, and the countryside. Yet the threats to purity authors perceived were not exclusively urban; they permeated all aspects of existence, even finding their way into the womb to foreordain lasciviousness in the unborn.

The surest way to locate perdition's path is to be led there. Among the most effective guides, according to advice literature, were prostitutes, themselves both sensuality's victims and its agents. They plied their trade freely in cities, enticing to doom naïve young men seeking their fortune, as well as catering to hardened libertines. But, John Harvey Kellogg pointed out, the "social evil" *had spread beyond city limits; there was scarcely a place in the whole land safe from the prostitute's sinister wiles.*

Illicit intercourse has been a foul blot upon humanity from the earliest periods of history.[1] At the present moment, it is a loathsome ulcer eating at the heart of civilization, a malignant leprosy which shows its hideous deformities among the fairest results of modern culture. Our large cities abound with dens of vice whose *habitués* shamelessly promenade the most public streets and flaunt their infamy in the face of every passer-by. . . .

In smaller cities, as well as in large ones, in fact, from the great metropolis down to the country village, the haunts of vice are found. Every army is flanked by bands of courtesans. Wherever men go, loose women follow, penetrating even to the wildness of the miner's camp, far beyond the verge of civilization.

So blatant and disturbing was prostitution that it attracted much scandalized assessment in print. In 1832 a young New York clergyman, the Reverend John McDowall, published a compendium of his investigations into the problem. His findings were so sensational and so thoroughly documented that they brought charges of depravity upon the pious Reverend McDowall. Ostensibly designed to warn youth away from prostitution and prostitutes, such nineteenth-century studies of "the social evil" *marked primitive attempts at surveying sexual habits with a semblance of precision. Dr. William W. Sanger's* The History of Prostitution: Its Extent, Causes, and Effects Throughout the World *(1858) included interviews with prostitutes and tables summarizing such detailed information about them as their ages, places of birth, and even their educational achievements. To the much maligned prostitute, then, belongs a measure of credit for inspiring some of the earliest empirical sex research in America.*

❧

Ladies of easy virtue were not the only persons capable of leading one astray. Young women, for their part, had to beware of the man of loose morals whose greatest delight was in dragging innocent females to his own level of sensuality. William Andrus Alcott described the type for masculine readers whom he hoped to discourage from predatory activities. Like many male authors, Alcott tempered his denunciations of seducers with a sense that disgraced females generally deserved their fate.

In nineteen cases out of twenty, of illicit conduct, there is perhaps, no seduction at all; the passion, the absence of virtue, and the crime, being all mutual.[2] But there are cases of a very different description. Where a young man goes coolly and deliberately to work, first to gain and rivet the affections of a young lady, then to take advantage of those affections to accomplish that which he knows must be her ruin, and plunge her into misery for life—when a young man does this, I say he must be either a selfish and unfeeling brute, unworthy of the name of man, or he must have a heart little inferior, in point of obduracy, to that of the murderer. Let young women, however, be aware; let them be *well* aware, that few, indeed, are the cases in which this apology can possibly avail them. . . .

The most direct injury against the spiritual nature of a fellow being is, by leading him into vice. I have heard one young man, who was entrusted six days in the week to form the immortal minds and hearts of a score or two of his fellow beings, deliberately boast of the number of the other sex he had misled. What can be more base? And must not a terrible retribution await such Heaven daring miscreants? Whether they accomplish their purposes by solicitation, by imposing on the judgment, or by powerful compulsion, the wrong is the same, or at least of the same nature; and nothing but timely and hearty repentance can save a wretch of this description from punishment, either here or hereafter.

Unlike the prostitute, or the heartless seducer, other potential corruptors lurked within the family circle itself. Nineteenth-century Irish immigration provided a pool of inexpensive female servant labor, willing to work in middle-class homes. This allowed prosperous parents to delegate a substantial portion of child-raising to domestics; for large parts of the day a nurse was available to act as a mother's replacement—a discomforting situation to numerous moralists, Dr. Joseph W. Howe among them.

At least ninety per cent of the persons addicted to the vice [of masturbation] owe their misfortune to the instructions obtained from domestics or from older and more vicious playmates.[3] Or they are taught by erotic nurses in whose care they are placed by confiding parents. A gentleman of my acquaintance, who for years suffered from the consequences of onanism, informed me that his first experience occurred between five and six years of age. The nurse, who slept in his room, carried him one night to her own bed, and gave him his first lesson in the art, a lesson which cost him years of feeble health, anxiety and pain. His case is only one in thousands. It shows that the character and habits of the nurse and domestic have often more to do with the future welfare of the child than the character and habits of the parents. All nurses, good, bad, and indifferent, need watching.

Howe was wrong to dismiss the parents' role so quickly. They too could help the child take his or her first halting steps toward depravity, a fact Dr. Kellogg made manifest to his readers.

LIBIDINOUS BLOOD. In no other direction are the effects of heredity to be so distinctly traced as in the transmission of sensual propensities.[4] The children of libertines are almost certain to be rakes and prostitutes. History affords numerous examples in illustration of this fact. . . .

Is it unreasonable to suppose that the abnormal passion which led David to commit the most heinous sin of his life in his adultery with Bathsheba and subsequently procuring the death of her husband, was really a hereditary propensity which had come down to him through his ancestors, and which, under more favorable circumstances, was more fully developed in his sons? The trait may have been kept dormant by the active and simple habits of his early years, but asserted itself in full force under the fostering influence of royal idleness and luxury. In accordance with the known laws of heredity, such a tendency would be the legitimate result of such a combination of circumstances. . . .

Physiology shows conclusively that thousands of parents whose sons have become libertines and their daughters courtesans, have themselves implanted in their characters the propensity which led them to their unchastity.

If parents did not betray their children genetically, they still might do irreparable moral damage in the weeks preceding conception, at the time of conception, or during gestation. Dr. John Cowan explained the dreadful possibilities.

If the parents desire a child that will be the embodiment of licentiousness, it is only necessary that during these periods of preparation [for procreation] and influence [gestation]—beside eating of rich food and using hot drinks, alcoholic liquors and tobacco—they practice the abnormally amative of their natures—that they together lead incontinent lives—that they put to shame the beasts of the field in their unnatural lust.[5] By doing this they will not fail to have children whose unnatural desires will crop out very long before they have reached manhood or womanhood—long before their bodies are so grown and perfected as to be prepared to take on the holy duties and responsibilities of a loving and pure married existence. Think you I harp too much on this theme of the abnormal exercise of amativeness, and especially at these seasons of the birth and growth of a new life? You cannot so think, if you are of an observing and reflecting nature. Ask any discreet, watchful and observing male or female teacher of any one of the primary schools in town or country, and you will be told that the practice of self-abuse is next to universal in children; that it is practiced by girls as well as boys; that children before they reach the age of five years practice it—practice it in company and alone; that these children, as they grow up, become pale, weak and sickly—caused, as the fond parents suppose, by hard study; that eventually many of these young men become insane, while others die of some unpronounced disease—consumption or general debility—when *the* cause of death was the body-disintegrating, soul-destroying habit of self-abuse. And the great underlying cause for the practice of self-abuse in the child was the fact that it was transmitted by the parents, during some one or other of these seasons of pre-natal influence. . . .

Live a licentious married life, and you cannot possibly expect to have children that will be other than licentious and incontinent.

Cowan's scheme of things, like Kellogg's and like that of so many other advice-manual authors, had the effect of placing upon parents the most exacting responsibilities for securing their children's moral purity, and the most excruciating sense of failure for their children's transgressions.

The battle was not won merely because a person was fortunate enough to evade the depraving influences of prostitutes, seducers, nurses, and parents. Sociability had its perils as well, and so did some of the most sacred artifacts of middle-class life, including education and books.

Dr. Elizabeth Blackwell notified parents that there was more to examine than academic excellence when selecting a school for children. There were, it appears, unforeseen consequences to nineteenth-century educational institutions.

The material arrangements and regulations, as well as the moral tone of any school to which a child is sent, must be considered.[6] It being remembered that the vices of self-abuse and fornication are the great curses of our schools and colleges, the means must be sought for, by which these vices can be as rigidly excluded from our educational establishments as the vice of thieving; school and college sentiment should be taught to regard them as equally dishonorable and unmanly. They must be overcome chiefly by moral agencies, in connection with hygienic arrangements. It is a false and cruel delicacy which ignores this great danger, and sends an innocent child, utterly unprepared, into a corrupt school society. The views of the head of the school on the subject of sexual education, the character of assistant teachers, the water-closet and sleeping arrangements, the amount of outdoor exercise, and the character of the moral influence brought to bear on the pupils, must be carefully studied by the conscientious parent.

Corruption by one's peers was not confined to schools and colleges. The rolling eloquence of Henry Ward Beecher—God's thunder itself—reverberated against sinister friendships and other mountains of debauchery.

I warn the young of evil companions.[7] Decaying fruit corrupts the neighboring fruit. You cannot make your head a metropolis of base stories, the ear and tongue a highway of immodest words, and yet be pure. Another, as well as yourself, may throw a spark on the magazine of your passions; beware how your companions do it. No man is your friend who will corrupt you. An impure man is every good man's enemy—your deadly foe; and all the worse, if he hide his poisoned dagger under the cloak of good fellowship. Therefore, select your associates, assort them, winnow them, keep the grain, and let the wind sweep away the chaff. . . .

But I warn you, with yet more solemn emphasis, against EVIL BOOKS and EVIL PICTURES. There is in every town an undercurrent which glides beneath our feet, unsuspected by the pure; out of which, notwithstanding, our sons scoop many a goblet. Books are hidden in trunks, concealed in dark holes; pictures are stored in sly portfolios, or trafficked from hand to hand; and the handiwork of depraved art is seen in other forms which ought to make a harlot blush. . . .

Upon the plea of exhibiting nature and man, novels are now scooped out of the very lava of corrupt passions. They are true to nature, but to nature as it exists in knaves and courtesans. Under a plea of humanity, we have shown up to us troops of harlots, to prove that they are not so bad as purists think; gangs of desperadoes, to show that there is nothing in crime inconsistent with the noblest feelings. . . . Exhausted libertines are our professors of morality. They scrape the very sediment and muck of society to mould their creatures; and their volumes are monster-galleries in which the inhabitants of old Sodom would have felt at home as connoisseurs and critics. . . . This black-lettered literature circulates in this town, floats in our stores, nestles in the shops, is fingered and read nightly, and hatches in the young mind broods of salacious thoughts.

Lorenzo Fowler (one of several phrenological Fowlers) would have added a hearty "amen" to Beecher's indictment of nineteenth-century literature. Fowler's own critique came while he listed "causes of the perversion of amativeness." *For good measure he added a popular form of amusement omitted in Beecher's tirade.*

[Among the common inspirations to sensuality is:] . . . reading works of romance written by persons of morbid feelings, sickly sentiments, and extravagant hopes—all containing highly wrought scenes of amatory happiness and earthly felicity—thus exciting the animal feelings and weakening the judgment, creating a distaste for commonplace transactions, and giving false and imperfect ideas of human nature. . . .[8]

[Also causing corruption is the practice of:] . . . attending theatres and other similar places of amusement, whose principal attractions are, unnatural and far-fetched representations of scenes overloaded with "love," in sentiment and in action, the most absurd, because unreal. In truth, it may well be called *acting*. Besides, at these places there are resorts where licentiousness stalks openly and defyingly, where the most abandoned congregate, a moral Upas tree, which disseminates all impurity and blights with deadly and destructive effect the moral feelings.

Fowler's venture in drama criticism had good reason behind it. In the 1840s a few New York theatres featured performances giving the illusion of nudity, if not more. In 1848, following police raids, a newspaper mourned the loss of

Those nice *tableaux vivants*
Of beautiful young ladies, *sans*
Both petticoats and pants,
Who scorning fashion's shifts and whims,
Did nightly crowds delight,
By showing up their handsome limbs
At fifty cents a sight.[9]

Whatever empirical basis there was to Fowler's perception of the arts in nineteenth-century America, he was not alone in his fears. William Andrus Alcott went beyond Beecher and Fowler in searching out corrupting influences.

The world abounds in impure publications, which almost all children (boys especially), at sometime or other, contrive to get hold of, in spite of parental vigilance. . . .[10]

The same remarks might be extended, and with even more justice, to licentious paintings and engravings, which circulate in various ways. And I am sorry to include in this charge not a few which are publicly exhibited for sale, in the windows of our shops. You may sometimes find obscene pictures under cover of a watch-case or snuff box. In short, there would often seem to be a general combination of human and infernal efforts to render the juvenile thoughts and affections impure; and not a few parents themselves enter into the horrible league. . . .

Many persons, and even not a few intelligent parents, seem to think that a loose or immoral song cannot much injure their children, especially if they express their disapprobation of it afterwards. . . .

It is painful to think what errors on this subject are sometimes tolerated even by decent society. I knew a schoolmaster who did not hesitate to join occasional parties (embracing, among others, professedly Christian parents), for the purpose of spending his long winter evenings, in hearing songs from a very immoral individual, not a few of which were adapted to the most corrupt taste, and unfit to be heard in good society. Yet the community in which he taught was deemed a religious community; and the teacher himself prayed in his school, morning and evening! Others I have known to conduct [themselves] even worse, though perhaps not quite so openly.

I mention these things, not to reproach teachers, for I think their moral character, in this country, generally, far better than their intellectual, but as a specimen of perversion in the public sentiment; and also as a hint to all who have the care of the young. Pupils at school, cannot fail to make correct inferences from such facts as the foregoing.

DOUBLE ENTENDRES.* By this is meant seemingly *decent speeches, with double meanings*. I mention these because they prevail, in some parts of the country, to a most alarming degree; and because parents seem to regard them as perfectly harmless. Shall I say—to show the extent of the evil—that they are sometimes heard from both parents? Now no serious observer of human life and conduct can doubt that by every species of impure language, whether in the form of hints, innuendos, double entendres, or plainer speech, impure thoughts are awakened, a licentious imagination inflamed, and licentious purposes formed, which would otherwise never have existed. . . .

* Pronounced *entaunders*. [Alcott's note]

Evening Parties. One prolific source of licentious feeling and action may be found, I think, in evening parties, especially when protracted to a late hour. It has always appeared to me that the injury to health which either directly or indirectly grows out of evening parties, was a sufficient objection to their recurrence, especially when the assembly is crowded, the room greatly heated, or when music and dancing are the accompaniments. Not a few young ladies, who after perspiring freely at the latter exercise, go out into the damp night air, in a thin dress, contract consumption; and both sexes are very much exposed, in this way, to colds, rheumatisms, and fevers.

But the great danger, after all, is to reputation and morals. Think of a group of one hundred young ladies and gentlemen assembling at evening, and under cover of the darkness, joining in conclave, and heating themselves with exercise and refreshments of an exciting nature, such as coffee, tea, wine, &c, and in some parts of our country with diluted distilled spirit; and "keeping up the steam," as it is sometimes called, till twelve or one o'clock, and frequently during the greater part of the night. For what kind and degree of *vice,* do not such scenes prepare those who are concerned in them?

Advice manual authors were right. Nineteenth-century society did contain its share of moral perils—prostitutes, lechers, depraved servants, licentious parents, debasing schools, evil companions, pornography, lewd music, and other instruments of corruption. But then every century is filled with what its moralists regard as perils of one sort or another. A late seventeenth-century Puritan minister would have lamented in his day some of the same inducements to depravity nineteenth-century writers found in theirs, give or take a few peculiarly fashionable sins. More singular, however, were the menaces nineteenth-century authors located within each individual's control: a person's habits, his tastes in food, his body itself could betray him into sin. One not only had to move carefully through a world of snares and delusions, one also had to keep a watchful eye on the enemy within, on the corrupted (or merely uninformed) heart. There were patterns of personal behavior, easily fallen into, which promised to unleash sexuality from the tightly circumscribed area to which proper morality confined it.

Even choice of career, according to Dr. Frederick Hollick, had serious moral consequences. Dr. Hollick drew upon the Annual Reports of the Massachusetts State Lunatic Asylum to buttress his startling revelations.

Another valuable fact also shown in these reports is the influence of occupation in leading to solitary vice.[11] It is proved conclusively that light sedentary employments very much favor the formation of such habits, and that on the contrary active out-of-door occupation has the contrary effect. Thus among "merchants, printers, students, and shoemakers," *fifty per cent* of the insanity arises from masturbation, and only *twelve per cent* from intemperance; while among carpenters, blacksmiths, and others who are actively employed, *thirty-five per cent* of the insanity arises from intemperance and only *thirteen per cent* from masturbation. Among seamen again *fifty-four per cent* of the insanity arises from intemperance, and only *eleven per cent* from solitary vice. These facts should be duly weighed by parents when choosing employment for their sons. Many a youth of sanguine temperament, urgently requiring muscular and mental occupation of the most varied kind, is condemned to the monotonous inactivity of a counting-house desk, the distasteful plodding of an office or some merely intellectual profession, and in consequence becomes listless, dogged, and self-debased. In such cases the abundant vital energy, that ought to have been expended in active exertion, is retained, and, by stimulating the sexual organs to an unnatural degree, leads to solitary vice both as a gratification and a relief.

[*With a touch of professional pride, Dr. Hollick noted:*] I can find physicians made insane by other causes, but neither in [the thirteenth] Report, nor in the one for the preceding year, do I find *a single case* of one becoming insane from masturbation!

Choices still more intimate than that of occupation had their dangers as well. "Clothes make the man" and "hair is a woman's crowning glory" are old expressions, given special meaning in nineteenth-century advice manuals like Dr. Cowan's The Science of a New Life.

The great provocative of amative desires in woman, next to a wrong quality and quantity of food, is dress.[12] The constricting of the waist and abdomen by corsets, girdles and waistbands, prevents the return of the venous blood to the heart, and the consequent overloading of the sexual organs, and, as a result, the unnatural excitement of the sexual system. In the mode of wearing the hair, it is observable that the majority of women, adoring followers of the goddess Fashion, wear the hair in a large, heavy knot on the back part of the head, and when their own is insufficient to make a roll large enough, false hair is added. This great pressure of hair on the small brain produces great heat in the part, and causes an unusual flow of the blood to amativeness, and, if persisted in, a chronic inflammation of the organ, and a chronic desire for its sexual exercise. . . .

The fashionable women, or the imitators of such, who wear corsets, long dresses, and a pile of false or natural hair, covering that part of the brain in which amativeness is located, will take as naturally to a life of sexual excess—legitimate or otherwise—as would a whiskey-steeped, tobacco-flavored male sensualist. Such a woman cannot possibly lead a continent life, and it is almost impossible, in the nature of things, that she should lead other than a life of sexual excess.

Nineteenth-century writers like Cowan have not been alone in associating style of dress and length of hair with immorality. Cowan and his peers, however, were remarkable for giving their prejudice the cloak of scientific "fact," thanks (in Cowan's case) to a mixture of phrenology and physiology. But occupation and appearance are external matters, relating to social pressures and to the figure one cuts in the world. Advice-manual authors also believed what went on inside mind and body to be of great significance for sexual purity.

"Think no evil," was another homily given rapturous endorsement by various authorities, Henry Ward Beecher for one.

I solemnly warn you against indulging a *morbid imagination.*[13] In that busy and mischievous faculty begins the evil. Were it not for his airy imaginations, man might stand his own master, not overmatched by the worst part of himself. But ah! these summer reveries, these venturesome dreams, these fairy castles, builded for no good purposes—they are haunted by impure spirits, who will fascinate, bewitch, and corrupt you. *Blessed are the pure in heart.* Blessed art thou, most favored of God, whose THOUGHTS *are chastened,* whose imagination will not breathe or fly in tainted air, and whose path hath been measured by the golden reed of Purity.

John Harvey Kellogg was less metaphorical about wandering thoughts—and wandering eyes.

It is vain for a man to suppose himself chaste who allows his imagination to run riot amid scenes of amorous associations.[14] The man whose lips delight in tales of licentiousness, whose eyes feast upon obscene pictures, who is ever ready to pervert the meaning of a harmless word or act into uncleanness, who finds delight in reading vivid portrayals of acts of lewdness—such a one is not a virtuous man. Though he may never have committed an overt act of unchastity, if he cannot pass a handsome female in the street without, in imagination, approaching the secrets of her person, he is but one grade above the open libertine, and is as truly unchaste as the veriest debauchee.

Man may not see these mental adulteries, he may not perceive these filthy imaginings; but One sees and notes them. They leave their unclean scars upon the soul. They soil and mar the mind; and as the record of each day of life is photographed upon the record books in Heaven, they each appear in bold relief, in all their innate nastiness.

Other nasty habits served to draw men (and, more rarely, women) into sensuality. Dr. Hollick outlined one of them.

Tobacco is an article that exerts a most decided action, in numerous cases, upon the generative organs, though few persons suspect it of doing so.[15] Like opium, and some other narcotics, it often stimulates at first, but afterwards greatly weakens the sexual power, so as to bring on complete impotence in many cases. I am satisfied, from my own observations, that it frequently leads to involuntary emissions, and keeps them up notwithstanding all that can be done for them. Many young men, patients of mine, have remarked that a cigar at bed-time would be certainly followed by emission before morning, and they found it necessary in consequence to abandon its use. . . .

I could, in fact, give numerous cases, both among single and married, showing the effects of this poisonous drug, and I do not hesitate to say that I think it has more to do with many [sexual] complaints than has been hitherto supposed.

It was here, on the subject of ingestion, that virtue's nineteenth-century sentinels were most unusual. Sylvester Graham certainly did not invent the idea that particular foods and beverages produce lustful desires while other foods and beverages moderate the passions: such claims appeared in literature and folklore well before him. But in the 1830s the quixotic Graham began extensive promotion of proper diet as a cure for disease, both moral and physical, and his regimen had a vigor and detail earlier formulations lacked. Faddish though Graham's program was, its basic tenets nevertheless passed into respectable medical literature and stayed there long after Graham's name had fallen into oblivion. The connections Graham made between diet and sex do not exist (at least not in the way he made them); but his program itself did speak to one real issue—Americans of his day ate appallingly large amounts of appallingly prepared food, just as their descendants do.

The delicate susceptibilities of youth being constantly tortured, and their young blood continually heated by a *stimulating and depraving diet,* their sensual propensities are much more rapidly developed than are their rational and moral powers; and a preternatural excitability of the nerves of organic life is inevitably induced; while other habits of luxury and effeminacy serve to increase the general debility of their system, and assist in throwing a common anarchial depravity over the whole of the instincts. . . .[16]

Among the causes of extensive and excessive self-pollution . . . the most important are—

1. Improper diet—the free use of flesh, with more or less stimulating seasonings and condiments, together with coffee, tea, rich pastry, and compounded and concentrated forms of food; and too often, chewing and smoking tobacco, and drinking wine and other intoxicating liquors; all of which unduly stimulate and irritate the nervous system, heat the blood, and early develop a preternatural sensibility and prurience of the genital organs.

2. Excesses in quantity of aliment. Were our children kept in the plainest and simplest manner, unless they were restrained as to quantity by their parents or guardians, they would be exceedingly apt to eat more than they really need, and more than the vital economy of their bodies can dispose of without oppression and irritation. But subsisting, as most children do, on a variety of dishes, variously and often viciously prepared—too generally warm, and requiring little mastication, they are sure to eat too rapidly, and swallow, in a very imperfectly masticated condition, far too great a quantity of food. This not only produces permanent injury in the digestive organs, but the whole constitution is much impaired by it, and the sexual appetite rapidly developed and strengthened. *Over-feeding is a powerful cause of early concupiscence and licentiousness, as well as of innumerable other evils;* and it is an almost universal fact in our country, that children are greatly over-fed. Hundreds are annually destroyed by this means.

[*Graham listed lack of exercise, overstimulation of the brain, obscene conversation, lewd books, and corrupt companions as the other prominent causes of "self-pollution."*]

Dr. Frederick Hollick compiled a convenient list of foods available for men wishing to curb (or to restore) sexual powers.

Some kinds of food stimulate the sexual organs while other kinds have the contrary effect upon them.[17] Shell-fish . . . are usually stimulating, owing to the phosphorus they contain, but other fish have no such power. Flesh-meat is stimulating merely because it is nutritious, but it is a great mistake to suppose that it is of necessity more so than vegetables. There are some vegetables that are often more stimulating than flesh, especially those that are *farinaceous* or contain much starch, as the potato for instance, which, when of good quality, contains most of the elements the body needs. Most strong tasted or aromatic vegetables have a stimulant effect, such as Celery, Parsnips, Onions, and *Asparagus,* especially, and so have all seasoning herbs, such as Mint, Sage, Pennyroyal, and Thyme. Spices and condiments have a still stronger action, especially the Peppers and Nutmeg. Mushrooms stimulate some people very much, and Truffles still more, and even Olives exert a marked influence at times. The flesh of birds I think is not stimulating, except that which is red, such as ducks and geese. I have several times been assured that eating freely of the *Canvass-back duck,* when in season, has been highly beneficial to those who were weakened by excess, probably partly from its own nature and partly from the wild Celery on which it feeds. Of all meats, however, *Turtle* has the greatest reputation for exciting the generative organs, and I think with good reason. It is undoubtedly highly nutritious, and it appears also to contain some *heating* principle, which specially affects those parts.

As a general rule all watery vegetables, such as turnips, cabbage, and squash, have no such effect as those enumerated, and are therefore proper when we wish to keep down excitement. Acid fruits also come under the same category, and indeed fruits generally, except some highly flavored ones, such as peaches, and pine-apples which are undoubtedly *aphrodisiac,* except they disagree with the stomach.

Tomatoes are rather stimulating, and so are most kinds of beans, especially the Lima Beans, but peas are not so. Wheaten bread or wheaten flour in any form, is more stimulating than the flour of any other grain, while Indian meal is probably the least so. When we desire an anaphrodisiac effect therefore, Indian bread should be used, with mush, samp or hominy, instead of wheaten bread or potatoes. Rice is unstimulating, but sago, tapioca, and arrow-root are the reverse.

In regard to drinks it may be stated that all alcoholic liquors are highly stimulating when first taken, but they soon lose their power if used too long or intemperately, and then they become injurious. . . . Coffee is almost as stimulating as wine, and should never be used by those who are disposed to involuntary emissions, nor by those whose desires are too strong. Tea is different from coffee in this respect, and is therefore the better drink in such cases. Milk, though highly nutritious, is not stimulating and it therefore forms an excellent drink for those who are disposed to emissions or exciting dreams.

Psychological theory since Freud has dealt with interrelationships between sexual drives and attitudes toward food and excrement. Graham's theories, and their modification by later writers, do nothing to discredit such associations. Abstinence from exciting diet became, in advice books, synonymous with chastity; control of bowels became, for some writers, equivalent to control of erotic impulses. "In males," *Dr. Kellogg wrote,* "one of the most general physical causes of sexual excitement is constipation." [18] *Dr. Hollick had decided quite the contrary—that constipation leads to sexual weakness. But the point was much the same: regulation of one bodily function implied regulation of others, just as mortification of one appetite (whether for food or sex) meant mortification of others.*

⁂

If we are to believe nineteenth-century advice books, morality required eternal vigilance. Seducers of all sorts threatened to pull men and women into vice and eventual destruction—seducers who stood brazenly on street corners, entered the family circle, lurked in classrooms and dormitories, or lay waiting between handsomely printed covers. But morality demanded even more than coping with a menacing society; a virtuous human being also had to come to terms with incitements to sensuality residing in the most intimate details of personal behavior, even in things so essential as the body's demand for nourishment.

Probably few people could maintain the constant anxiety advice literature called for, and advisers themselves were really at a very old and thankless task, despite the new form it had taken. Like their Puritan clerical forebears, they tried to guide their contemporaries through a world riddled with pitfalls. Also like their Puritan forebears, nineteenth-century advisers called for introspection, urging men and women to look for evil within, as well as to beware of the world's temptations. By the nineteenth century, however, the authorities were secular, and the inward corruptions were not just of the heart but of all the viscera, and both sins and retribution were biological as well as theological.

---

1 J. H. Kellogg, *Plain Facts about Sexual Life* (Battle Creek, Mich.; The Office of the Health Reformer, 1877), p. 199.

2 William A. Alcott, *The Young Man's Guide,* 16th ed. (Boston: T. R. Marvin, 1846), pp. 306, 311–312.

3 Joseph W. Howe, *Excessive Venery, Masturbation, and Continence* (New York: Bermingham & Company, 1883), p. 64.

4 Kellogg, *Plain Facts,* pp. 205–207.

[5] John Cowan, *The Science of a New Life* (New York: Cowan & Company, 1880), pp. 210–11, 214.

[6] Dr. Elizabeth Blackwell, *Counsel to Parents on the Moral Education of Their Children* (New York: Brentano's Literary Emporium, 1879), pp. 114–15.

[7] Henry Ward Beecher, *Twelve Lectures to Young Men, on Various Important Subjects,* rev. ed. (New York: D. Appleton and Company, 1879), pp. 154–57.

[8] L. N. Fowler, *Marriage: Its History and Ceremonies; With a Phrenological and Physiological Exposition of the Functions and Qualifications for Happy Marriages* (New York: Fowler and Wells, Publishers, 1853), p. 83.

[9] Quoted in Milton Rugoff, *Prudery and Passion* (New York: G. P. Putnam's Sons, 1971), p. 264.

[10] Alcott, *Young Man's Guide,* pp. 330–33, 335, 337.

[11] Frederick Hollick, *The Male Generative Organs in Health and Disease, from Infancy to Old Age,* 120th ed. [sic.]. (New York: n.d.), pp. 331, 330, Hollick delivered anatomical lectures, probably those upon which this book was based, in the 1840s.

[12] Cowan, *Science of a New Life,* pp. 99–100, 366.

[13] Beecher, *Twelve Lectures,* p. 154.

[14] Kellogg, *Plain Facts,* pp. 94–95.

[15] Hollick, *Male Generative Organs,* pp. 289, 291.

[16] Dr. Sylvester Graham, *Chastity, in a Course of Lectures to Young Men; Intended also, for the Serious Consideration of Parents and Guardians* (New York: Fowler and Wells. Publishers, n.d.), pp. 9, 34–35.

[17] Hollick, *Male Generative Organs,* pp. 349–51.

[18] Kellogg, *Plain Facts,* p. 114.

CHAPTER FOUR

Woman, Sensuous and Otherwise

The Victorian lady, icily aloof from all dangerous impulses, loomed like a white-clad mountain amid the world's moral debris. She was (legend has it) an asexual creature, regarding sensuality with disgust and reproduction as a necessary evil. There were, however, Victorian women, wanton sorts who appeared in memoirs of libertines, on the pages of nineteenth-century pornography, and on police blotters. No matter how they regarded sensuality, they catered to it; reproduction was either a consequence they sought to avoid or an activity they engaged in with abandon. Ethereal and earthy—these were femininity's counter-images.

Reality lay elsewhere, in more complex and compelling lives; but stereotypes of women had their function in advice literature, particularly because female sexuality proved a riddle to nineteenth-century authorities. Male erotic impulses were easily comprehended: writers commonly assumed that man's passions were fierce, always boiling just beneath the surface. Diverted and repressed (their very existence questioned), woman's sexual urges moved in more mysterious ways. Although most advice manuals dealt at greater length with male than with female erotic drives, what these books had to say about being female and about woman's fate is fully as significant as more prominent topics and is ultimately more ambiguous than the cardboard stereotypes behind which discourse often hid.

Nineteenth-century authors were capable of producing inspired rubbish and sublime nonsense on most subjects, but on none more than on womanhood. Many discussions drifted into transcendental rhapsodies, virtually losing all sight of earthly beings. William H. Holcombe's The Sexes Here and Hereafter (1869) gave warning of such tendencies as early as the author's dedication, which was "To MY MOTHER and MY WIFE, who Above All OTHERS, HAVE CONTRIBUTED TO EXALT AND SPIRITUALIZE MY CONCEPTION OF WOMAN." So thoroughly spiritualized was Holcombe's conception that he managed to speak of sexual relations for 277 pages without betraying a sense that woman had any biological functions whatsoever. The result, however, was less unique in advice literature than was Holcombe's method of achieving it. Holcombe, a physician profoundly inflenced by Emanuel Swedenborg, the Swedish mystic, did not deny sexuality but simply discovered it everywhere. Delighting in the "great principle of sexuality, flowing from the dual nature of God himself," Holcombe believed that masculinity and femininity were all around him, even in language. "The letters of the alphabet have their sexes," Holcombe proclaimed. "The vowels are feminine and the consonants are masculine elements of speech." [1] The effect was to make female and male sexuality so abstract as to be virtually meaningless.

Few writers matched Holcombe's imagination or his comprehensiveness, yet all would have agreed that sex differences were not merely biological but also permeated human personality and moral sensibility. "Woman's perception of virtue is generally understood to be more nice than that of men," wrote William G. Eliot, Jr., accurately reporting a cliché.[2] Nelson Sizer, marking sexual differences from a phrenological perspective, quoted with full approval a contemporary's description of woman. "Woman is more pure, tender, affectionate, and patient than man," Sizer's source claimed. "She is the counterpart of man—taken out of man, to comfort him like angels and to lighten his cares. She thinks less profoundly than man; sensibility is her power." [3] Virtue and sensibility implied removal from sensual impulses—if one accepted the prevalent belief that sex was a part of animal nature, impure when indulged freely. Here complexities of female sexual response and a fashionable image of woman clearly reinforced each other. Woman's apparently cooler passions signified an inherent chastity and, therefore, an inherent moral refinement superior to man's.

Presumption of woman's chronic virtuousness even informed studies focusing on females who did not fit the mold. Dr. William Sanger found, to his distress, that over one-fourth of the prostitutes he interviewed said they entered their profession voluntarily, out of "inclination." Sanger strove manfully to reconcile his data with his view of woman's character.

In itself such an answer would imply an innate depravity, a want of true womanly feeling, which is actually incredible.[4] The force of desire can neither be denied nor disputed, but still in the bosoms of most females that force exists in a slumbering state until aroused by some outside influences. No woman can understand its power until some positive cause of excitement exists. What is sufficient to awaken the dormant passion is a question that admits innumerable answers. Acquaintance with the opposite sex, particularly if extended so far as to become a reciprocal affection, will tend to this; so will the companionship of females who have yielded to its power; and so will the excitement of intoxication. But it must be repeated, and most decidedly, that without these or some other equally stimulating cause, the full force of sexual desire is seldom known to a virtuous woman. In the male sex nature has provided a more susceptible organization than in females, apparently with the beneficient design of repressing those evils which must result from mutual appetite equally felt by both. In other words, man is the *aggressive* animal, so far as sexual desire is involved. Were it otherwise, and the passions in both sexes equal, illegitimacy and prostitution would be far more rife in our midst than at present.

Denials of strong female sexuality formed part of an image of woman that ultimately proved confining, even degrading; but in the nineteenth century there were no necessarily pejorative implications to statements that women possessed less erotic energy than men. Influential figures in the Woman's Rights movement, in fact, sometimes made the point with pride. Sarah M. Grimké, informing a correspondent that women were naturally superior to men, based her judgment in part on a faith that "the sexual passion in man is ten times stronger than in woman."[5] *Such assertions often justified a sexual double standard, which permitted males their transgressions while insisting that proper females cling to chastity. Although that conclusion achieved some popularity in nineteenth-century society, authors of advice manuals were unwilling to draw it. Quite the contrary, they maintained that woman's sensibility, being more elevated than man's, represented the ideal by which both sexes ought to be judged. Dr. Elizabeth Blackwell felt there was no room for doubt on the matter.*

The great truth now to be recognized, is the fact, that male as well as female purity is a necessary foundation of progressive human society.[6]

This important subject must no longer be ignored. The time has come for its acceptance by all experienced men and women. The necessity of upholding one moral standard as the aim to be striven for, must become a fundamental article of religious faith.

Dr. Blackwell allowed both men and women to share in elimination of licentiousness. Other authors with reformist sympathies occasionally came to a harsher conclusion, one reflected at times in the Woman's Rights movement: woman's nature qualified her, rather than man, to control sexual expression; inborn purity should predominate over male lust. Dr. John Cowan listed among woman's prerogatives:

. . . the right to her own person.[7]

The violation of this last "right" by the man and husband, whose existence centres in the animal, and the sensual pleasures that come of perverted amativeness, has done more for woman's debasement, degradation and misery, than has the violation of all the other "rights."

Cowan's book bore with it endorsements from William Lloyd Garrison, the abolitionist, and Elizabeth Cady Stanton, pioneer in the Woman's Rights movement. They, and other reform-minded men and women, took the doctrine of innate female purity to a startling extreme: if women were particularly qualified to rule on moral matters then they ought to be able to take the lead in social reformation, exercising their power through public agitation and the ballot box. More conservative individuals could see no such implication, believing that women flourished in the home, withered in the crass atmosphere of business and politics, and achieved their greatest influence through a mother's dominion over her children and husband. Whatever conclusions one derived from the idea of woman's natural chasteness, the idea itself met few challenges.

❧

There were females who refused to behave with the purity expected of their sex. "Woman is, by nature, far more chaste than man, in the present state of the world;" *Sylvester Graham wrote, adding ruefully,* "but it is *possible* to deprave even woman."[8] *Preeminence has its perils—those who fall from it fall farthest, and a female who lost her virtue was, if anything, more reprehensible than a male who did; she went against her nature while he only obeyed his. In moral dramas fashioned by advisers like William G. Eliot, Jr., there were no roles for women other than angel of light or painted lady.*

Of all the influences in society, calculated to purify and elevate man's character, that of virtuous and well educated women is perhaps the strongest.[9] From the hallowed precincts of the domestic circle, it drives away all sinful pleasure; in the intercourse of social life, it makes virtue attractive and sin hateful. It touches the soul to its gentler issues, and bestows a grace upon whatever is noble in human life. . . .

But in proportion as she [woman] exerts a good and purifying influence, when well educated and virtuous, her influence becomes pernicious, if her character is perverted. When frivolous or heartless, she turns many from good; when wicked, she is the most successful minister of ruin. The best things perverted, become the worst. Take from the air we breathe, one of its component parts, and a single breath of it causes death. Take from woman's character her love and practice of virtue, and her presence becomes death to the soul.

The depths of female depravity, so nightmarish to contemplate, inspired as much hyperbole as did the heights of female virtue. Henry Ward Beecher, with his skill for lurid rhetoric, warned young men of* "Strange Women," *waiting to entice them into sin.

I. Can language be found which can draw a corrupt beauty so vividly as this: *Which forsaketh the guide of her youth, and forgetteth the covenant of her God?* [10] Look out upon that fallen creature whose gay sally through the street calls out the significant laugh of bad men, the pity of good men, and the horror of the pure. . . . Alas, *she forsook the guide of her youth!* Faint thoughts of evil, like a far-off cloud which the sunset gilds, came first; nor does the rosy sunset blush deeper along the heaven, than her cheek at the first thought of evil. Now, ah, mother, and thou guiding elder sister, could you have seen the lurking spirit embosomed in that cloud, a holy prayer might have broken the spell, a tear have washed its stain! Alas, they saw it not! She spoke it not; she was *forsaking the guide of her youth.* She thinketh no more of heaven. . . .

II. The next injunction of God to the young is upon the ensnaring danger of beauty. . . .

If God hath given thee beauty, tremble; for it is as gold in thy house; thieves and robbers will prowl around and seek to possess it. If God hath put beauty before thine eyes, remember how many strong men have been cast down wounded by it. . . .

III. In the minute description of this dangerous creature [the

"Strange Woman"], mark next how seriously we are cautioned of her WILES.

Her wiles of dress. Coverings of tapestry and the *fine linen of Egypt* are hers; the perfumes of *myrrh and aloes and cinnamon.* Silks and ribbons, laces and rings, gold and equipage; ah, how mean a price for damnation! . . .

Her wiles of speech. . . . What horrid wizard hath put the world under a spell and charm, that words from the lips of a STRANGE WOMAN shall ring upon the ear like tones of music; while words from the divine lips of religion fall upon the startled ear like the funeral tones of the burial-bell! Philosophy seems crabbed; sin, fair. Purity sounds morose and cross; but from the lips of the harlot words drop as honey and flow smoother than oil; her speech is fair, her laugh is merry as music. . . .

Her wiles of LOVE. . . .

Simple man, trust not thyself near the *artful* woman, armed in her beauty, her cunning raiment, her dimpled smiles, her sighs of sorrow, her look of love, her voice of flattery; for if thou hadst the strength of ten Ulysses, unless God help thee, Calypso shall make thee fast, and hold thee in her island.

Next, beware the wile of her *reasonings. To him that wanteth understanding she saith, Stolen waters are sweet, and bread eaten in secret is pleasant. I came forth to meet thee, and I have found thee.*

What says she in the credulous ear of inexperience? Why, she tells him that sin is safe; she swears to him that sin is pure; she protests to him that sin is innocent. . . .

I will point only to another wile. When inexperience has been beguiled by her infernal machinations, how, like a flock of startled birds, will spring up late regrets and shame and fear; and, worst of all, how will conscience ply her scorpion-whip and lash thee, uttering with stern visage, "Thou art dishonored, thou art a wretch, thou art lost!" . . .

These wholesome pains, not to be felt if there were not yet health in the mind, would save the victim, could they have time to work. But how often have I seen the spider watch, from his dark round hole, the struggling fly, until he began to break his web; and then dart out to cast his long, lithe arms about him, and fasten new cords stronger than ever. So, God saith, the strange woman shall secure *her* ensnared victims, if they struggle. . . .

She is afraid to see thee soberly thinking of leaving her and entering the path of life; therefore her ways are movable. She multiplies devices, she studies a thousand new wiles, she has some sweet word for every sense. . . .

IV. Having disclosed her wiles, let me show you what God says of the chances of escape to those who once follow her: *None that go unto her return again, neither take they hold of the paths of life.* The strength of this language was not meant absolutely to exclude hope from those who, having wasted their substance in riotous living, would yet return; but to warn the unfallen into what an *almost* hopeless gulf they plunge, if they venture. . . . There are . . . evils which hold men to them, because they are like the beginning of a fire; they tend to burn with fiercer and wider flames, until all fuel is consumed, and go out only when there is nothing to burn. Of this last kind is the sin of licentiousness; and when the conflagration once breaks out, experience has shown what the Bible long ago declared, that the chances of reformation are few indeed. The certainty of continuance is so great, that the chances of escape are dropped from the calculation; and it is said, roundly, NONE THAT GO UNTO HER RETURN AGAIN.

Beecher's bombast may reveal more about male fears of female seductiveness than about actual women, strange or otherwise. He made no mention of possible redemption for the temptress—her sinfulness was absolute; yet there was hope that fallen men might, with arduous effort, extricate themselves from her evil snares. There was more here than concern for New York city's prevalent prostitution—especially because Beecher's villainess was portrayed in such a way that she could have been any erotically stimulating female. Lurking in denunciation of the STRANGE WOMAN *is evidence that the doctrine of female purity, pressed to its logical limits, could only make its believers uncomfortable when faced with real women who betrayed signs of sensuality. This does not mean that proper nineteenth-century women never displayed erotic impulses; undoubtedly many couples found satisfactory sexual expression with each other. Yet continual harping on woman's instinctive chastity obviously circumscribed both masculine and feminine responses to female eroticism.*

Disgust with female sexuality went beyond being a mere convention, to be elaborated upon by professional moralists like Henry Ward Beecher. The rhetorical castigation "sinful" females received from advice manuals was mild compared to diagnoses and treatment dispensed by quite sober medical men. Dr. Augustus K. Gardner, Professor of Clinical Midwifery at the New York Medical College, was scarcely more flattering in gauging female depravity than was Beecher.

Far less common, indeed, is [masturbation] among females than among the male youth; perhaps, too, less disastrous in its results to the mental and physical economy; yet much of the worthlessness, lassitude and physical and mental feebleness attributable to the modern woman are to be ascribed to these habits as their initial cause.[11]

Gardner undoubtedly had in mind two types of women familiar in nineteenth-century literature—the invalid, suffering from a mysterious but unfathomable languorousness, and the hysterical female. He may even have been perceptive in attributing their maladies to sexual disturbance; but repression and guilt were far more likely culprits than autoeroticism.

Dr. Gardner and his colleagues were ready to prescribe stern measures for curing "unhealthy" forms of sexual expression in women, including juvenile masturbation (which they were excessively hasty to classify as nymphomania). Dr. Charles Meigs, authority on Woman: Her Diseases and Remedies, *related a particularly grim instance he dealt with to his own satisfaction.*

Case of Nymphomania. I have met with a few samples of this terrible malady in the course of my long experience, and I am thankful to be able to say, but few; and those, not of the greatest intensity.[12] In one of the cases, which occurred in a thin brunette, aged only nine years, I learned to my astonishment, that for months she had been in the almost constant habit of irritating the erotomaniac sense by various methods of provoking its exaltation, while at school on the form, or standing up in class, at church, at table, in the dining parlor, and more than all upon retiring to bed; so that it appeared, she was very rarely without the sexual sense in a highly exalted state. Her health had become feeble, and from the most ingenuous and gentle of children, she had grown cunning, deceitful, and wicked in disposition.

I made vain efforts, through moral treatment, to awaken the compunctions of conscience, and to set in array the dictates of common sense, and the love of life and health. The affair became so threatening that it was necessary to examine the parts, which were natural in appearance. . . .

I put the case under a severe course of purgative medicines, that were repeated for a long time, and rendered her thin and weak. I gave purgatives to the child in order to reduce her strength by diminishing the crasis of the blood, hoping that such a cooling operation might be followed by some diminution of the erotic excitement.

I also directed ten grains of nitrate of silver, dissolved in one ounce of water, to be procured. The solution was freely applied to the nymphae and clitoris for several successive days. The child declared she had abandoned her habit, grew fatter and stronger; but at length confessed she had always continued in secret to excite her sexual sense.

She was finally sent to the country, when her health became strong, and I have reason to believe that she lost her frightful propensity upon the recovery of her health. What, indeed, is ever likely to render all the innervations natural and healthful, if a firm and solid health of all the other organs fail to conduct back to a normal nutrition an organ or tissue that has become disordered. Health, like mercy, is twice blessed, since it not only gives to the organs, which is blessing, but receives from them, which is blessing also. I am not, therefore, surprised, when I learn that a case so distressing, recovered under the invigorating influence of fine air and exercise, which, by restoring the harmonious concurrence of the other innervations, compelled those of the aphrodisiac tissues to come under the same law of harmony. . . .

There should be in your therapeutical and hygienical views, as to the disorder under consideration, I think, a constant intention to build up, as early as possible, the shattered edifice of the nervous system by good air and a nourishing, but simple and not stimulating diet; by exercise, carried to the extent of turning off every excess of nerve power in the direction and activation of the muscular system; by an almost constant presence; by new, innocent, and attractive trains of occupation and thought; and the employment of the ferruginous tonics and vegetable bitters; the shower-bath; cold hip-bath; sleeping under thin coverings, and doubtless, above all, the administration in the evening of a full dose of opium by enema.

Dr. Joseph Howe, writing a generation after Meigs, was less inclined to identify masturbation with nymphomania; but he regarded female sexual drives with a professor of clinical surgery's coldly disapproving eye.

NYMPHOMANIA, sometimes called furor uterinus, is a disease peculiar to females.[13] It often arises from masturbation, or excessive sexual indulgence. It has also been known to occur from the sudden cessation of such pleasures. Sometimes it manifests itself in healthy young women who have never masturbated, and who are innocent of any practical knowledge of the sexual relations. Such persons are naturally passionate, and their unsatisfied desires, their continence, is the real exciting cause of the affection.

Nymphomania is apt to occur between the ages of sixteen and twenty-five. Blondes are more frequently subject to it than brunettes. It is characterized by an uncontrollable appetite for lascivious pleasures, exhibited (in its worst forms) in public and private, without regard to time, place, or surroundings. In mild cases the patient is nervous, easily excited, subject to hysterical attacks, and is constantly exciting herself in various ways to provoke an orgasm. The mind is full of lascivious ideas which find vent in self-pollution. While there is any modesty left, the patient deceives everyone with regard to the true state of her feelings. She will invent numberless diseases to account for her condition, and for the purpose of being manipulated by the surgeon. Every disease that necessitates an examination of the genitals will in turn be taken up. . . .

The only cure for the affection is marriage, or amputation of the clitoris, according to the plan recommended by Baker Brown, who has reported numerous cures by the operation. In this connection it may be well to mention that Dr. Brown incurred the enmity of his professional brethren for a too free use of the operation in this as well as allied affections, and was, I think, compelled to leave some of the London medical societies, of which he was a prominent member.

Suggestions that marriage might be a cure for excessive sexual desire were angrily rejected by most authors of advice literature, but Howe was far from unusual in his endorsement of drastic measures, including clitorectomy, for females who displayed erotic drives.

Although physicians like Dr. Meigs and Howe were quick to prescribe, female sexuality posed greater diagnostic problems than they acknowledged. How could a creature so pure as woman become, at times, vile enough actually to exhibit symptoms of lust? Meigs, Howe, and their colleagues scarcely bothered to search for explanations in their zeal to get on with the cure—the evil's existence was enough of a fact for them. Others simply seized upon the most obvious formula: men corrupted women, even though, once corrupted, woman might in turn lure man into depravity. But nineteenth-century authorities possessed a curiosity and an intellectual vigor which frequently outran their prejudices, and some of them searched about for explanations that were at least partly sociological.

Moral judgments of all sorts shaped Dr. William Sanger's survey of New York prostitutes, yet the questions his investigators were instructed to ask, and the way Sanger categorized answers, revealed a reasonably open attempt to uncover the true forces impelling women who took to the streets. The following is Sanger's summary of responses to the most crucial question of all:

QUESTION. What was the cause of your becoming a prostitute? [14]

Causes	*Numbers*
Inclination	513
Destitution	525
Seduced and abandoned	258
Drink, and the desire to drink	181
Ill-treatment of parents, relatives, or husbands	164
As an easy life	124
Bad company	84
Persuaded by prostitutes	71
Too idle to work	29
Violated	27
Seduced on board emigrant ships	16
Seduced in emigrant boarding house	8
Total	2000

Although presuming (perhaps correctly) that prostitution correlated with emigrant status, liquor, and corruption by others, Sanger's questionnaire nevertheless tacitly acknowledged that female sexual behavior might not be innately determined, but rather, in some degree, might be at the mercy of such social and cultural forces as poverty and peer group pressure. Some of the same attitudes filtered into Dr. Elizabeth Blackwell's Counsel to Parents, *twenty years later. Dr. Blackwell saw prostitution partly as a matter of scarce economic opportunities (a point made by members of the Women's Rights movement); yet, going even farther, she grasped an interaction between female sexuality and class.*

The customs of civilized nations practically consider poor women as rightful subjects for a life so dishonorable, that a rich man feels justified in ostracizing a wife, sister, or daughter, who is guilty of the slightest approach to such a life.[15] The great mass of poor women are often regarded as the subjects to be used for the benefit of the upper classes. Young and innocent men, it is true, fall into vice, or are led into it, or are tempted into it by older women, and are not deliberate betrayers. But the Rubicon of chastity once passed, the moral descent is rapid, and the preying upon the poor soon commences. The miserable slaves in houses of prostitution are the outcasts of the poor. The young girls followed at night in the streets are the honest working-girl, the young servant seeking a short outdoor relief to her dreary life, as well as the unhappy fallen girl, who has become, in her turn, the seducer.

If, fearful of health, the individual leaves the licensed slaves of sin, and the chance associations of the streets, it is amongst the poor and unprotected that he seeks his mistress: the young seamstress, the pretty shop-girl, the girl with some honest employment; but poor, undefended, needing relief in her hard-working life. It is always the poor girl that he seeks. She has no pleasures, he offers them; her virtue is weak, he undermines it; he gains her affection and betrays it; changes her for another and another, leaving each mistress worse than he found her, farther on in the downward road, with the guilt of fresh injury from the strong to the weak, on his soul. Any reproach of conscience—conscience, which will speak, when an innocent girl has been betrayed, or one, not yet fully corrupted, has been led farther on in evil life—is quieted by the frivolous answer, "They will soon marry in their own class." If, however, this sin be regarded in its inevitable consequences, its effects upon the life of both man and woman, in relation to society, the nature of this sophistry will appear in its hideous reality. Is chastity really a virtue? something precious in womanhood? then the poor man's home should be blessed by the presence of a pure woman. Does it improve a woman's character to be virtuous? Has she more self-respect in consequence? does she care more for her children, for their respectability and welfare, when she is conscious of her own honest past life? Does she love her husband more? and will she strive to make his home brighter and more attractive to him; exercising patience in the trials of her humble life; being industrious, frugal, sober, with tastes that center in her home?

These are vital questions for the welfare of the great mass of the people; consequently of society and of the nation.

We know, on the contrary, as a fundamental truth, that unchastity unfits a woman for these natural duties. It fosters her vanity; it makes her slothful or reckless; it gives her tastes at variance with home life; it makes her see nothing in men but their baser passions, and it converts her into a constant tempter of those passions—a corrupter of the young. We know that drunkenness, quarrels, and crimes have their origin in the wretched homes of the poor; and the center of those unhappy homes is the unchaste woman, who has lost the restraining influence of her own self-respect, her respect for others, and her love of home.

When a pretty, vain girl is tempted to sin, a wife and mother is being ruined; discord and misery are being prepared for a poor man's home, and the circumstances created out of which criminals grow. Nor does the evil stop there. It returns to the upper classes. Nurses, servants, bring back to the respectable home the evil associations of their own lives. The children of the upper classes are thus corrupted, and the path of youth is surrounded at every step with coarse temptations. . . .

The growth of habits of licentiousness amongst us, exerts the most direct and injurious influence on the lives of virtuous young women of the middle and upper classes of society. The mode of this influence demands very serious consideration on the part of the parents. It is natural that young women should wish to please. They possess the true instinct, which would guide them to their noble position in society, as the centers of pure and happy homes. How do our social customs meet this want? All the young women of the middle and upper classes of society, no matter how pure and innocent their natures, are brought, by these customs of society, into direct competition with prostitutes! The modest grace of pure young womanhood, its simple refined tastes, its love of home pleasures, its instinctive admiration of true and noble sentiments and actions, although refreshing as a contrast, will not compare for a moment with the force of attraction which sensual indulgence and the excitement of debauch exert upon the youth who is habituated to such intoxications. The virtuous girl exercises a certain amount of attraction for a passing moment; but the intense craving awakened in the youth for something far more exciting than she can offer, leads him ever farther from her, in the direction where this morbid craving can be freely indulged.

Many strands come together in Dr. Blackwell's analysis. Proper lady and uncouth prostitute once again faced each other, opposites and opponents, yet unacknowledged sisters—both of them products of a moral code and a social structure which excluded sensuality from the world of decency. Dr. Blackwell was perceptive enough to glimpse how beliefs about woman's erotic nature helped pattern relations between classes and between sexes. But her insights also included ambiguities which she shared with other, less acute authorities. She was critical of conventional sexual practices; and yet she wrote from within orthodox moral assumptions, not seeing that so severe an emphasis on chastity encouraged illicit contact between middle-class males and degraded females—because sex could only be sought openly with social inferiors, or with admittedly depraved women. Equally typical, Dr. Blackwell placed woman's influence largely within home and family (rather surprisingly, when her own career as a physician had come after fierce struggle against those who wished to deny women a place outside the home). Dr. Blackwell, of all people, should have seen the crowning irony here. Woman, thought to be the least sensual of human beings, was assigned marriage and family as her proper sphere of action—the institutions designed to regulate sexuality. Dr. Blackwell, a female and a physician, was better qualified than anyone else to know that both the institutions, and the sexual assumptions behind them, bound womanhood to inhuman standards of purity or else sentenced it to shame and condemnation.

---

1 William H. Holcombe, *The Sexes Here and Hereafter* (Philadelphia: J. B. Lippincott & Co., 1869), p. 29.

2 William G. Eliot, Jr., *Lectures to Young Women,* 5th ed. (Boston: Crosby, Nichols, and Company, 1855), pp. 32–33.

3 Nelson Sizer, *Thoughts on Domestic Life, Its Concord and Discord. With Suggestions How to Promote the One and Avoid the Other.* (New York: Fowlers and Wells, Publishers, 1850), p. 15.

4 William W. Sanger, *The History of Prostitution: Its Extent, Causes, and Effects Throughout the World* (New York: Harper & Brothers, Publishers, 1858), pp. 488–89.

5 Sarah M. Grimké to [Elizabeth Smith Miller], June 1, 1873, Weld MSS, the Clements Library, University of Michigan.

6 Dr. Elizabeth Blackwell, *Counsel to Parents on the Moral Education of Their Children* (New York: Brentano's Library Emporium, 1879), p. 105.

7 John Cowan, *The Science of a New Life* (New York: Cowan & Company, Publishers, 1880), p. 381.

8 Dr. Sylvester Graham, *Chastity, in a Course of Lectures to Young Men; Intended also, for the Serious Consideration of Parents and Guardians* (New York: Fowler and Wells, Publishers, n.d.), p. v.

9 William G. Eliot, Jr., *Lectures to Young Men* (St. Louis: Republican Office, 1852), pp. 78–79.

10 Henry Ward Beecher, *Twelve Lectures to Young Men, on Various Important Subjects,* rev. ed. (New York: D. Appleton and Company, 1879), pp. 136–44.

11 Augustus K. Gardner, *The Conjugal Relationships as Regards Personal Health and Hereditary Well-Being, Practically Treated,* 5th ed. (Glasgow: Thomas D. Morison, 1905), p. 69.

12 Charles D. Meigs, *Woman: Her Diseases and Remedies. A Series of Letters to His Class* (Philadelphia: Blanchard and Lea, 1859), pp. 151–52.

13 Joseph W. Howe, *Excessive Venery, Masturbation, and Continence* (New York: Bermingham & Company, 1883), pp. 108–11.

14 Sanger, *History of Prostitution,* p. 488.

15 Blackwell, *Counsel to Parents,* pp. 65–68, 72, 73.

CHAPTER FIVE

Marriage...

According to nineteenth-century morality, sex, like womanhood, was to be chained by wedlock's bonds. But sexual expressiveness was not to be left to a married couple's discretion. Unlike present-day advisers, who commonly preach mutual fulfillment and pleasure, nineteenth-century authorities emphasized restraint of erotic drives, even in matrimony. Consequently, much sounds outmoded in their essays on the erotic questions posed by marriage and mate choice. Nevertheless, in pursuit of answers, nineteenth-century advisers discovered trails which, after many twistings and turnings, eventually led toward contemporary conventional wisdom about marital compatibility.

◆§ §◆

Mason Locke Weems made both his reputation and much of his living as a purveyor of platitudes. Born in Maryland in 1759, he was an Episcopal clergyman who turned to literary pursuits in the 1790s. Weems' enduring reputation, such as it is, rests largely upon a laudatory biography of George Washington which perpetrated the legend that the young future president could not tell a lie, even about chopping down a cherry tree. The Life and Memorable Actions of George Washington *did not, however, exhaust Weems' literary or moral energies. Between 1799 and his death in 1825, he ground out tracts assuming courageous stands against murder, gambling, drunkenness, duelling, adultery, and shrewish wives. Among the earliest of these was* Hymen's Recruiting-Sergeant; Or the New Matrimonial Tat-Too for Old Bachelors, *which first appeared around 1799. Although remaining in print until the middle of the nineteenth century,* Hymen's Recruiting-Sergeant *looked backward to the eighteenth century, when patriots like Benjamin Franklin considered reproduction and population growth as matters for American pride, not for dire concern. Weems, also like Franklin before him, regarded marriage and sex as subjects to be treated with a mixture of bluff humor and practicality, as the opening passages of his pamphlet amply reveal:*

I AM very clear that our *Yankee Heroes* are made of, at least, as good stuff as any the best of the beef or frog-eating gentry on t'other side of the water.[1] But neither this, nor all our fine speeches to our President, nor all his fine speeches to us again, will ever save us from the British gripe or Carmagnole hug, while they can outnumber us, *ten to one!* No, my friends, 'tis population, 'tis *population alone,* can save our bacon. . . .

And the Lord said, *"It is not good for the man to be alone."*—Gen. ii.15.

No, verily, nor for the woman neither. But, what says the preacher? Why, "I will," says Paul (and Paul, you know, was a sound divine) "that the young women marry, and love their husbands; and raise up good children." 'Tis well said, most noble, patriotic Paul! May the children of Columbia hearken to thy counsel! that there be no more old Bachelors in our land, like scrubby oaks, standing selfishly alone, while our maidens, like tender vines lacking support, sink to the ground; but that, united in wedlock's blest embraces, they may grow up together as the trees of the Lord, whose summits reach the skies, and their branches overspread the nations, making their country the pride and glory of the earth!

Weems proceeded to enumerate the various blisses of matrimony, most of which were profoundly utilitarian. Marriage, for instance, "increases the pleasure of defraying family expenses," " 'Tis the only money making state," *and* "preserves a young man from that worse than hellish practice, duelling." *The only overtly sexual issue, as far as Weems was concerned, was supremely practical and could be faced squarely. Matrimony, Weems asserted,* "preserves youth from the harlot's clutches."

For all its longevity in print, Hymen's Recruiting-Sergeant *was an anachronism after 1820, a vestige of days when sex and marriage were discussed genially and shrewdly, and when erotic activity promoted American glory rather than individual destruction. In contrast, some of Weems' nineteenth-century successors smothered the topic in senti-*

mentality while others proved far grimmer about marriage and sex than either the jovial Parson Weems or their own transcendental contemporaries. At the extreme of airy and elevated sensibility was William H. Holcombe, the Swedenborgian physician.

Marriage is the great civilizer of man; the organizer of society; the peace-giver and joy-giver of the world.[2] Its condition among a people is the true measure of their spirituality. If all men and women were married and their marriages were perfect, wars would cease; diseases would disappear; supreme order would prevail; love universal would reign; heaven would descend to earth.

If such be the origin, nature, and effects of marriage, why should it cease with this life? If sex is spiritual and love is spiritual and marriage is spiritual, why should they not also be eternal? Who is to divorce the two souls that have been wrought into one by the unitizing operation of God's own law? Are there recognitions and reunions in the Happy Land for parents and children, for brothers and sisters, for friends and neighbors? and shall they whose souls and bodies have been made one by divine institution, whose beings are knit together by the sweetest, holiest, profoundest sympathies—shall they meet each other merely as neighbors and know each other merely as friends? Impossible! Why should the conjugial love alone perish?—conjugal love, the foundation of all other loves, and itself the first and sweetest gift of God! . . .

Verily, sex, love and marriage are eternal. . . .

The sexuality of man and woman consists really in the sexual differences between their souls, which are thence anatomically represented in their bodies. It is said in the Scripture that God created man male and female, in his own image and likeness. Surely the image and likeness of God is not in the physical bodies of men and women! That image and likeness must be found, if anywhere, in some male and female principles of the soul itself. Sex therefore is spiritual. If spiritual, it is eternal. Love is the attraction, the very life of the sexes; marriage is their union, their eternal life, their heaven.

Holcombe articulated a hope few men dare hold—for sex after death. With considerable understatement he added that his "spiritual philosophy of sex, so clear, so beautiful, so consonant with intuition and reason, and having such a sound scientific basis, is quite a new thing to the psychologies and theologies of the present day." *His philosophy was also so spiritual it made sexuality an abstraction rather than an activity and marriage so holy that copulation nearly vanished in mists of rhetoric. Perhaps—in Holcombe's defense—there was no other way to preserve genteel conventions and yet make Eros acceptable to proper consciences.*

In contrast to Dr. Holcombe, a greater number of nineteenth-century genteel consciences were firmly convinced that Eros had gained an unfortunate predominance in marriage. Prostitution and secret vice were chilling enough, but—as disturbing to some advisers—sensuality seemed to have infiltrated matrimony, creeping into the very institution entrusted with regulating sexual impulses in a culturally sanctioned way. Dr. John Cowan explained the appalling process to his readers.

It is a common belief that a man and woman, because they are legally united in marriage, are privileged to the unbridled exercise of amativeness.[3] This is wrong. Nature, in the exercise of her just laws, recognizes no human enactments, and is as prompt to punish any infringement of her laws in those who are legally married as in those out of the bonds. Excessive indulgence between the married produces as great and lasting evil effects as in the single man or woman, and is nothing more or less than legalized prostitution.

Dr. Russell Trall was willing to excuse a certain amount because of prevalent ignorance, but he was fully as concerned by the dangers marital excess posed as was Cowan. (He also provided still another glimpse of the nineteenth-century woman-invalid; and, once again, suggested a sexual origin for her mysterious ailment.)

The majority of young persons unite in matrimony with no education whatever on this subject [sexual intercourse]; and habits, right or wrong, are soon formed which are apt to be continued through life.[4] I have had patients who had for years indulged in sexual intercourse as often as once in twenty-four hours, and some who have indulged still oftener. Of course the result was premature decay, and often permanent invalidism. It was not because these persons were inordinately sensual, or unusually developed in the cerebellum, that they damaged themselves in this way. It was simply because they knew no better. Many a man who would have been a good husband if he had only known how, and who would not for his life, much less for the momentary pleasure it afforded, have endangered the health, or hazarded the happiness of a well-beloved wife, has destroyed her health, happiness and life (some men several wives successively) by excessive sexual indulgence.

Married men are not always as sensual in character, nor as cruel in disposition, as they seem. With many sexual intercourse becomes a habit, like eating, working and sleeping; and they indulge in it with nearly the same regularity that they do in their other habits, reckless and thoughtless of its consequences to themselves or their wives. And it is no uncommon thing for the physician to attend an invalid woman for years whose ailments are chiefly attributable to this habit on the part of her husband. Almost every physician of large practice has a circle of "everlasting patients" whom he visits and prescribes for once a week, on the average, for years; who never get much better at home, but always improve at once when removed to a proper distance from their bosom companions. I do not charge their physicians with remissness in duty in not instructing both parties how to avoid the necessity of employing him professionally, for, generally, physicians are as heedless and as ignorant as the people are on this subject.

Marriage was a kind of sexual liberation for young men who had previously behaved chastely (contrary to their impulses). They—Dr. Augustus K. Gardner warned—were in for a rude awakening.

It would scarcely seem necessary to counsel husbands to be guided somewhat by reason instead of yielding themselves entirely to the control of their passions.[5] And yet such advice is requisite, and to none more so than to those who have been always distinguished for their correctness of conduct. Indeed, those who during early manhood have not been strict Josephs in their morality, whose passions have been somewhat calmed by indulgence, are usually less rash and extravagant in their demands. But he who has been hitherto restrained by his fears, or by high religious principle, from sexual indulgence, often thinks that now he is free morally and religiously to gratify his natural desires to their utmost, and forgets the limitations of the physical nature.

Excess in lawful desire is subject to the same corporeal laws as in unlawful, and its penalty is disease and debility. I have seen no more marked instances of physical and nervous debility and disorganisation than I have noted in young clergymen and in their virtuous wives. These imaginative men, of highly nervous temperaments, thoughtlessly anticipate a repayment for all past restraints, in unlimited physical gratification.

Despite such grim diagnoses, there were some contradictory voices, authorities who persisted in seeing marriage as therapy for various sexual complaints. Dr. Charles Knowlton, attempting to justify contraception, advocated the one socially approved form of intercourse to cure a common "disease."

In many instances the genital organs are rendered so irritable by the repletion to which unnatural continency gives rise, and by the much thinking [sic.], caused by such repletion, as to induce a disease known to medical men by the name of *Gonorrhoea Dormientium.*[6] It consists in an emission or discharge of the semen during sleep. This discharge is immediately excited in most instances by a lascivious dream, but such dream is caused by the repletion and irritability of the genital organs. It is truly astonishing to what a degree of mental anguish the disease gives rise in young men. They do not understand the nature, or rather, the cause of it. They think it depends on a weakness—indeed the disease is often called a "seminal weakness"—and that the least gratification in a natural way would but serve to increase it. Their anxiety about it weakens the whole system. This weakness they erroneously attribute to the discharges, they think themselves totally disqualified for entering into or enjoying the married state. Finally, the genital and mental organs act and react upon each other so perniciously, as to cause a degree of nervousness, debility, emaciation, and melancholy—in a word a wretchedness that sets description at defiance. Nothing is so effectual in curing this diseased state of body and mind in young men as marriage. All restraint, fear, and solicitude should be removed.

Yet authors and physicians who, like Knowlton, stressed the healing powers of marital intercourse, generally met stern reprobation from their colleagues. Dr. Cowan's displeasure at such advice was unequivocal.

Marriage is sometimes recommended as a remedy for this habit [masturbation], especially when it has so grown on the individual as to be difficult of treatment. . . .[7] The remedy, in its exercise, is much worse than the disease, beside involving in filthy and lustful associations the pure and clean nature of the new-made wife. The man practicing self-abuse, and lacking the force of will to adopt proper remedial measures, and daring to give his enervated, shrunken, almost lifeless soul to the purity, strength and beauty of a ripe womanhood, should, if God would exercise a special indication of His displeasure, be stricken from the crown of his head to the soles of his feet with palsy, and so make of him a living, yet a dead example to all whose thoughts lead them in the desire to marry as a remedy for this filthy and soul-debasing practice.

Dr. John Harvey Kellogg was equally adamant. "As a learned professor remarks, in speaking of woman," *Kellogg noted,* "who has a right to regard her as a therapeutic agent?" [8]

❧

Marriage, then, rather than containing sexuality within proper boundaries, provided insidious opportunities for erotic blight to contaminate the innocent. Dr. Cowan explained:

A man with great vital force is united to a woman of evenly balanced organization.[9] The husband, in the exercise of what he is pleased to term his "marital rights," places his wife, in a very short time, on the nervous, delicate, sickly list. In the blindness and ignorance of his animal nature he requires prompt obedience to his desires, and, ignorant of the law of right in this direction, thinking that it is her duty to accede to his wishes, though perhaps fulfilling them with a sore and troubled heart, allows him passively, *never lovingly,* to exercise daily and weekly, month in and month out, the low and beastly of his nature, and eventually, slowly but surely, to kill her. And this man, who has as surely committed murder as has the convicted assassin, lures to his net and takes unto him another wife, to repeat the same programme of legalized prostitution on his part, and sickness and premature death on her part.

There are women—strongly passionate and often diseased—who, like such men, are endowed with strong animal natures, who, when they marry, in the intense exercise of their lustful natures, soon reduce the husband to a standard that physically and mentally places him below the brute, and long before the fulfillment of his just allotment of time on earth, he too dies. The number of such women is very much smaller than is the number of men with like tendencies; but when women are diseased in this direction, they go much further than is possible with men. It is for this reason I advised, in a former chapter, in the choice of a husband or wife, the avoidance of widows or widowers, the death of whose partners was caused by other than accident or well-understood disease; for when such cases, at the last day, come before the bar of judgment, it will be found that these premature deaths were murders, and that these sensualists were murderers.

The exercise of abnormal amativeness is known in all its positive intensity by those newly married. The honeymoon is one nightly repetition of legalized prostitution, sinking the pure, high and holy into the low, debasing and animal. Think you, oh! new-made husband and wife, that in this you do right? that in this you elevate your better natures? that in this you find peace, strength and happiness? that in this you grow into that pure and holy passion akin to God in its exercise—the passion of love? Do not, I pray you, deceive yourselves; for in this exercise of the sexual part of your nature you lower your standard of body and soul; and, as for love, *no man or woman can possibly love or be loved who lives other than a life of strict continence.*

Although, as Cowan suggested, some wives might lead their husbands into erotic frenzy, such occurrences seemed rare and blame for excess usually rested upon males. Marital intercourse, in fact, often appeared in advice literature as exploitation practiced by man upon woman.

Proprietor of a noted water-cure establishment and friend of prominent reformers, Dr. Russell Trall was certain where the erotic balance of power presently lay in marriage, and was equally certain where it really ought to lie.

As no propensity is more abused and abnormal, as the world is now constituted, than that of amativeness, and as sexual intercourse has become in married life, to a very great extent, a mere habit, to be indulged whenever the *man* feels the inclination, it follows that woman must be degraded to a mere machine in all that pertains to her highest interest and holiest aspirations.[10]

Trall's argument led to radical conclusions—nothing less than a challenge to male domination.

Woman's equality in all the relations of life implies her absolute supremacy in the sexual relation. It is for her to nourish and sustain the new being; it is her health and life that are directly imperiled by being compelled to bear children when she is unfitted and unwilling for the sacred office; it is her happiness that is more especially destroyed when forced to bring into the world sickly and deformed children, who can be nothing but a torment to themselves, of no use to the world, and nothing but a grief and a shame to their parents. For these reasons it is her absolute and indefeasible right to determine when she will, and when she will not, be exposed to pregnancy.

Important members of the Women's Rights movement heartily concurred with Trall's logic. "Woman's degradation is in man's idea of his sexual rights," *Elizabeth Cady Stanton wrote to Susan B. Anthony in 1860.*[11]

There was a good deal of merit to the argument. Women did endure the painful, sometimes shameful, consequences of childbearing while possessing few legal or social defenses against man's willful hegemony.

Yet childbearing was no more painful and man's dominion no more absolute in nineteenth-century America than had been the case earlier. A combination of changes in social and cultural conventions in the late eighteenth and early nineteenth centuries increased authorities' sensitivity to sexual exploitation of married females. Birth control and a rising standard of living for the middle classes made children neither so inevitable nor so desirable as in times when a large family was less likely to impede upward mobility (or as in times when there was less upward mobility for a large family to impede). Nineteenth-century people simply did not have to have children, and might actually find them a considerable inconvenience. Furthermore, belief in innate female purity served to make fecundity less a virtue that it had been in Parson Weems' day; woman's glory, orthodox morality implied, lay in her moral sensibilities, not in the measure of her reproductive capacity. A consequence of these and other factors was that woman, her position in life far more defined by marriage than man's, came also to appear as marriage's chief victim, both because of legal disabilities matrimony brought upon her and because of danger and degradation sexuality exposed her to.

☙ ❧

Although modern writers commonly believe that a wide range of adjustments in marital intercourse is possible, nineteenth-century authors, fearing erotic excess wherever it might appear, allowed couples little latitude. If sexuality required ceaseless vigilance and control, it demanded rules and regulations even within marriage. Varying in their particular formulae, nineteenth-century advisers nevertheless shared a spartan sense of what would be permissible among spouses. Refusing to give counsel on sexual techniques (unlike present-day authorities), advisers such as Sylvester Graham promoted abstemious routines for husbands and wives.

It is . . . impossible to lay down a precise rule, which will be equally adapted to all men, in regard to the frequency of their connubial commerce.[12] But as a general rule, it may be said to the healthy and robust, it were better for you not to exceed, in the frequency of your indulgences, the number of months in the year; and you cannot habitually exceed the number of weeks in the year, without in some degree impairing your constitutional powers, shortening your lives, and increasing your liability to disease and suffering—if indeed you do not thereby actually induce disease of the worst and most painful kind, and at the same time transmit to your offspring an impaired constitution, with strong and unhappy predispositions.

Dr. John Cowan's comments on the subject of marital intercourse have particular interest because of his attempt to distinguish varieties of common practice as well as to advance his own "Law of Continence."

Ask a man of an overgrown and intensely perverted amativeness what he considers a right definition of continence, and he will tell you that having nightly intercourse with his wife is with him a law of necessity, and his definition of continence.[13] And there are thousands of men and women—and especially those newly married—who by nightly debauchery record this as their solution of the Law of Continence; but it is a solution that involves in it immensely disastrous results to the individuals' present and future welfare of soul and body.

Ask another man, with more moderate desires, and he will tell you that thrice, twice, or perchance once a week, entitles him, as he considers it, to be classed as a continent man.

Ask yet another man, who, though possessing the full requirement of amative desires, yet has reflected and been somewhat enlightened on the subject, and he may tell you that, in his opinion, a man entitled to be classed among the continent men is one who, like himself, has intercourse monthly or semi-monthly.

This is about as high as you can get in the popular definition of this law [of continence]. . . .

A true solution of this difficulty, and one having unperverted nature for its exponent, can be secured by establishing the periods at and between which woman should reproduce and bear offspring. . . .

The man and wife come together at this period with the desire for offspring; impregnation and conception follow, and from that time until the mother has again menstruated—which occurs after the weaning of the child, and which in duration extends to about eighteen or twenty-one months—*sexual intercourse should not be had by either husband or wife.*

"Do you mean that the man should have no sexual intercourse for twenty-one months?"

That is precisely what is meant—precisely what Nature intended. *This is the only true solution of God's divine law in the government of the reproductive element in mankind,* and no man, since the time of Adam, has in the remotest manner broken this law, but has in some measure suffered the just penalty attached to it.

Though twenty-one months is the limit fixed for a life of purity and strict continence between the man and wife, I believe in a yet further extension of time. The twenty-one months of reproductive effort, on the part of the mother, necessarily in a measure lowers her vital powers, and therefore, after weaning, she should be allowed at least from one year to fifteen months to rest and recuperate. This may not be required in a perfectly healthy woman, but healthy women being an exception, the rule holds good. This would create an interval of nearly three years in which no intercourse should be had by the husband or wife, and in those who faithfully observe this rule is found the only strictly continent of mankind.

Cowan was extreme in his prescription for marital safety and happiness, but not unique. Others, however, were more willing to permit some nonreproductive activity and Dr. Joseph Howe even managed to construct a novel argument concerning the relative safety of sexual expression in marriage and outside it.

The occurrence of seminal ejaculations three or four times a week from legitimate sexual congress [in marriage] will not be felt very much by a healthy man, while the same number of losses from masturbation or nocturnal pollutions will soon superinduce mental and physical debility.[14] Indeed there are many persons in robust health who indulge in daily intercourse with impunity, while others with perhaps equal stamina, lose flesh from two or three weekly pollutions. The reasons for this are obvious. One act is performed in accordance with the dictates of nature—the other is subversive and degrading. During sexual intercourse the expenditure of nerve force is compensated by the magnetism of the partner. In all cases, or almost all cases, there is some return of that nature, which prevents injury. The masturbator feels that his act degrades his manhood, while the man who indulges in legitimate [marital] intercourse is satisfied that he has fulfilled one of his principal natural functions. There is a healthy instinctive expression of passion in one case, an illegitimate perversion of function in the other. . . . Whenever sexual intercourse fails to produce its tonic effect, when, instead of exhilaration of spirits and clearness of intellect, there are depression, weakness, tremulousness, anxiety and diminished power of concentration, then the act is injurious and the intervals between each co-habitation should be lengthened. If these warnings of nature are disregarded, a disordered condition of mind and body similar to that which arises from onanism will soon appear.

In addition to counseling upon frequency of intercourse, some authorities refused to leave place and manner up to whim or impulse. Dr. Frederick Hollick's word on such matters was a shrewd mixture of practicality and physiology.

The *time* for sexual indulgence should be so chosen that the temporary excitement and after-exhaustion resulting from it, may not interfere with any of the bodily or mental functions, nor distress the system by necessitating too much effort during any needful exertion.[15] Ignorance of this important rule, and consequent neglect of it, very often leads to great inconvenience, and even serious mischief. Sexual indulgence just after eating is nearly certain to be followed by indigestion, even if it does not cause immediate vomiting, owing to the temporary loss of nervous power thereby produced, which arrests the action of the stomach. Just *before* eating also the same evils may follow, from the stomach being made so weak that digestion cannot properly commence, and the food consequently ferments. . . . It is true, that most men experience *stronger desire* for indulgence *immediately after* a full meal, particularly when stimulating drinks have been used, but this does not prove that they choose the best time. . . . Nor should the licentious furor produced by wine be in any way considered as the promptings of nature.

Upon the same principles it is obviously injudicious to seek indulgence just previous to any mental effort being made, because the vital energy will be too much exhausted to allow of such effort being made with advantage. Nor is it advisable immediately *after* any great mental effort, because it is injurious to have *two* causes of exhaustion in action at the same time. The same remarks also apply to *muscular exercise,* which should neither immediately follow nor closely precede sexual indulgence, for the reasons above given. In short the period chosen should be one when both body and mind can enjoy repose, at least for a short period, both before and after, and when none of the functions are likely to be disturbed.

Like Dr. Hollick, Dr. Russell Trall was not content to leave the details of intercourse up to the married couples.

Time for Sexual Intercourse. The usual habits of sexual intercourse are the worst that the nature of the case admits of, either for the good of the parties themselves or for the benefit of the offspring.[16] The time chosen is usually when darkness reigns over the earth, as though the act was one to be ashamed of (which is true in many cases), and the part of the night the evening, when, generally, both parties are in their worst bodily and mental conditions. A hard day's work, an indigestible supper, and sexual intercourse, afford the rationale of a multitude of diseases and infirmities on the part of the parents, and of deformities, eccentricities and monstrosities innumerable on the part of the offspring.

If children are to be begotten, or if that result is either desirable or possible, the sexual embrace should be had in the light of day. It is only then that the magnetic forces and the nervous system are in their highest condition of functional activity, and the body, refreshed by sleep, in its most vigorous condition. But it should not be the hurried act of the early morning, like a hasty meal before a day's work. It is better that it should never be indulged, either early in the morning or late in the evening, but that the time be selected and appropriated for the purpose. As no function in life is more important, and as the consequences of a single act may be the happiness or misery of a future being, it is worth a little time and preparation. Indeed, it is impossible to name any function for the proper performance of which more elaborate preparation should be made. Yet it is almost the only one for which no preparation is usually made. Surely, if sexual intercourse is worth doing at all, it is worth doing well. And it would not exalt its importance one iota above its real merits, if certain days were set apart, consecrated, to the conjugal embrace. It might be one day in seven, or one day in twenty, or more or less; or if the demands of business or the duties of life do not admit of the requisite leisure, opportunities should be chosen as they present themselves, when the parties are in their most composed and comfortable condition. The rule herein indicated is not so difficult to follow as might seem at first. It only requires that its paramount importance be appreciated, and a disposition enkindled to regard it. "Where there is a will there is a way."

Even with such precise calculations, the safest course was to make the way difficult and to curb the will as much as possible. Not satisfied with mere advice, John Harvey Kellogg called spacious Victorian domestic architecture into service to help couples achieve the erotic discipline proper marriage demanded.

Many writers make another suggestion which would certainly be beneficial to individual health; viz., that the husband and wife should habitually occupy separate beds.[17] Such a practice would undoubtedly serve to keep the sexual instincts in abeyance. Separate apartments, or at least the separation of the beds by a curtain, are recommended by some estimable physicians, who suggest that such a plan would enable both parties to conduct their morning ablutions with proper thoroughness and without sacrificing that natural modesty which operates so powerfully as a check upon the excessive indulgence of the passions.

There is little indication that people actually regulated their sexual habits to the degree Trall, Hollick, Kellogg, and many of their colleagues recommended. These authors themselves indicated as much by their Cassandra-like warnings that millions were not obeying physiology's (and God's) commands. But their advice has its own kind of relevance: it exhibits starkly many crucial assumptions applied to serious study of sexuality. To urge precise regulation was to believe that erotic drives were amenable to reason and that their effects followed laws which could be discovered through scientific thought. Sex was not merely a matter long settled by divine revelation, but rather was beginning to take its modern place as a biological drive, related to other bodily functions and thus falling under the curious scrutiny nineteenth-century men and women applied to natural phenomena.

Intense concern for marital behavior also had a direct social significance, one quite central to an alteration in the meaning of marriage in nineteenth-century America. In earlier times matrimony had not just expressed the wishes of two individuals; it had involved whole families in calculations regarding transmission of property and status (if there was any of either). The feelings of potential husbands and wives were important but had to fit into a larger set of negotiations conducted by parents and relatives. It marked a considerable change to emphasize, as nineteenth-century authorities did, that marital behavior ought to be controlled to insure the happiness and good health of spouses and their children. This focused attention upon a couple's relationship with each other, not on their families or positions in life, although these persisted as subjects for judicious consideration. Consequently, traditional standards imposed in mate choice gave way in the nineteenth century to measurements of a couple's compatability. And so, by a roundabout course, a new perception of erotic activity's role in marriage led to a new kind of interest in procedures for selecting somebody to marry. Marital-advice literature inevitably became mate-choice literature.

L. N. Fowler's counsel about picking marriage partners was both less material and more dogmatic than Parson Weems' had been a half century earlier. Though Weems seemed to feel that any decent male or female with decent financial prospects would do, Fowler (like most of his contemporaries) rooted mate choice in science and in reason-guided love. Where Weems' goals were national population increase and per-

sonal prosperity, Fowler's was that elusive thing called happiness. Where Weems could justify marriage as "the only money making state," *Fowler explicitly rejected mercenary calculations. Where Weems fought bachelorhood, Fowler battled matrimony begun for false motives. The differences between Fowler and Weems went beyond those of individual temperament—they were rooted in culturally and socially determined expectations about what men and women could do for each other (and to each other) in matrimony.*

In the name . . . of science, of humanity, of posterity, and of moral obligation, I say, no one has a right to marry unless he has the natural qualifications, mentally and physically; and has these functions properly guided by enlightened reason. . . .[18]

A great majority of the evils existing in domestic life, doubtless, arise from an ignorance of the laws that should regulate them; and, in consequence of this ignorance, the human race is made wretched.

In former days, this ignorance was winked at; but, now that the light is beaming forth from every page of nature's book, and [as] "those who may read" and understand, we are the less excusable for violating nature's laws, and more loudly called upon to follow this light, and to act accordingly.

Marriage is too often made a matter of *feeling,* and not enough of *reflection* and *judgment.* Many are influenced by no other motive when they marry than that of being *in love,* and are thus led by the blind impulses of their nature to form a union for life without any regard for consequences. It being the duty of every healthy and well organized person to form these matrimonial relations, in order to secure the greatest amount of happiness, it is equally our duty to understand the means to be used, so as to secure the greatest amount of happiness, not only to ourselves, but to our posterity. To the want of this knowledge, in connexion with disobedience of the laws of our nature, can be ascribed most of our domestic difficulties—such as divorces, quarrelling, fault-finding, jealousies, and murders, besides a long list of diseases which parents transmit to their children—thus increasing sorrow and suffering until premature death closes the scene. . . .

The old maxim, that "Love is blind," is too true: it certainly needs a guide—which guide we have in the intellect. . . .

Many show the contracted view they take of this subject, by the kind of companions they select, and the motives that guide them in their choice.

Many allow one motive, qualification, attraction, condition, or circumstance to bias them, regardless of all other circumstances.

The desire of wealth, joined with indolence, often points to a *fortune,* instead of a companion—thus showing that some prefer to gratify one of the lowest and most selfish feelings of their nature at the expense of all other considerations. . . .

Some have the motive of *conquest* alone in view—a motive which should never exist—while others are actuated by *ambition,* esteeming rank and honors as the greatest prize—a most unpleasant situation, unless a fortune accompanies the union—while others are influenced not so much by pure, strong, and proper attachments and the desire of a permanent settlement and home of their own, as by motives of curiosity, by desire of change, and to have the name of being married.

Rejecting such "contracted" views and hoping to encourage proper mate choice, Lorenzo Fowler and his fellow advice-manual authors made explicit many of the "natural" laws upon which rational marriage should rest. Given their belief that erotic activity was potentially destructive, writers felt particularly compelled to determine when marital relations might be begun with least damage to the human system. The answer given most typically betrayed a fear that Americans married younger than was good for them, a fear which neatly paralleled a simultaneous decline in the United States' birth rate and an increasing middle-class tendency to delay matrimony. Dr. Elizabeth Blackwell put the case in terms of female health—other authorities made it for both sexes, generally maintaining that men ought to be slightly older than women.

The large majority of marriages are made too early.[19] A young lady is thought to be getting *rather* old at 20, but at 25 she is already an old maid; and yet, as a general rule, before the age of 25, she is not prepared to enter on the marriage relation; it is only from 20 to 25 that the body attains its full vigor—that every part having acquired its due solidity, becomes capable of employing all its functions without injury to the individual, and with full benefit to society. Before that age, the character is not sufficiently formed, nor the experience of society wide enough, to render the individual capable of selecting her true partner. . . . But on the subject of incompatibility of character, though productive of so much unhappiness, of so much vice, in the marriage relation, I shall not dwell—for it is the physical condition which belongs especially to my subject. These early marriages *exhaust the vital energy of the mother.* The remarkable changes which childbearing produces in the economy, require the whole energy of a strong constitution to sustain them adequately—and the care of children, the superintendence of a household, can only be supported by the vigor of a mature woman. Our young girls too early married, are crushed by the undue burdens. Their beauty quickly fades, they are afflicted by bodily weaknesses and disease, and they become absorbed in domestic cares, which they are unable to rule with grace and dignity.

In order to defend the proposition that marriage should occur no earlier than a person's mid-twenties, writers had to distinguish sharply between mere ability to reproduce and the correct time of life to engage in reproductive activity—a difference of over a decade the way most authors calculated things. The result was reinforcement of the emerging nineteenth-century concept of adolescence as a separate and special stage in human development. According to Dr. Blackwell:

The marked distinction which exists between puberty and nubility should be here noted.[20] It is a distinction based upon the important fact, that a work of long-continued preparation takes place in the physical and mental nature, before a new faculty enters upon its complete life. Puberty is the age when those changes have taken place in the child's constitution which make it physically possible for it to become a parent, but when the actual exercise of such faculty is highly injurious. This change takes place, as a general rule, from fourteen to sixteen years of age. Nubility, on the other hand, is that period of life when marriage may take place without disadvantage to the individual and to the race. This period is generally reckoned, in temperate climates, for the man, at from twenty-three to twenty-five years of age. About the age of twenty-five commences that period of perfect manly vigor, that union of freshness and strength which enables the individual to become the progenitor of vigorous offspring. The strong constitution transmitted by healthy parents, between the ages of twenty-five and thirty-five, indicates the order of Nature in the growth of the human race.

The problem of finding a proper mate could not be resolved simply by determining the right age to go hunting, and so advisers compiled elaborate lists of qualifications and disqualifications. Drunkards and libertines were out—they would surely exhaust spouses and blight offspring. Pure-minded and temperate individuals were the only conceivable prospects. Hoping to narrow the field down even farther, phrenologists brought their curious pseudo-science into play and calculated the compatibility of potential partners by skull shape and by analyzing what "propensities" best got along with what other "propensities." Non-phrenological writers formulated criteria of their own;

some looked for harmonious differences while others counseled people to marry those similar to themselves. Dr. Cowan took the whole thing so seriously that he proposed using newspaper advertisements to discover spouses with the correct physical and moral credentials.[21]

On the subjects of marriage and mate choice, nineteenth-century authorities passed along much pompous misinformation—bad advice when judged against present-day standards. But it was good advice in its own social context. Sensitivity to marital erotic exploitation did foreshadow a healthy concern for the sexual rights of women and did turn people toward thinking of wedlock as a matter of personal adjustment between its participants, not as a property and status relationship. Furthermore, advice manuals promised to let men and women order and control marriage, the institution closest to them, and to order and control sex, one of mankind's most chaotic drives. Although based on a harsh, fearful, and repressive morality, such a promise could not help but appeal to human beings functioning in a world in which precious few things seemed firmly under order and control.

---

1 M. L. Weems, *Hymen's Recruiting-Sergeant; Or the New Matrimonial Tat-Too, for Old Bachelors* (1799; rpt., Hartford: S. Andrus and Son, 1845), pp. iii–iv, 1. Weem's readers, more classically educated than we are, knew Hymen as a god of matrimony, not as a bit of anatomy.

2 William H. Holcombe, *The Sexes Here and Hereafter* (Philadelphia: J. B. Lippincott & Co., 1869), pp. 56, 58, 86–87.

3 John Cowan, *The Science of a New Life* (New York: Cowan & Company, Publishers, 1880), p. 103.

4 R. T. Trall, *Sexual Physiology: A Scientific and Popular Exposition of the Fundamental Problems in Sociology* (New York: Miller, Wood & Co., 1867), pp. 243–44.

5 Augustus K. Gardner, *The Conjugal Relationships as Regards Personal Health and Hereditary Well-Being Practically Treated,* 5th ed. (Glasgow: Thomas D. Morison, 1905), pp. 76–77.

6 Charles Knowlton, *Fruits of Philosophy. An Essay on the Population Question,* 2nd new ed. (London: Annie Besant and Charles Bradlaugh, n.d. [1877?]), pp. 16–17. Knowlton obviously is not talking about what we know as gonorrhea.

7 Cowan, *Science of a New Life,* pp. 365–66.

8 J. H. Kellogg, *Plain Facts about Sexual Life* (Battle Creek, Mich.; Office of the Health Reformer, 1877), p. 157.

9 Cowan, *Science of a New Life,* pp. 103–104.

10 Trall, *Sexual Physiology,* pp. 202, 203.

11 June 14, 1860, in Theodore Stanton and Harriot Stanton Blatch, eds., *Elizabeth Cady Stanton as Revealed in Her Letters, Diary and Reminiscences,* Vol. II (New York: Harper & Brothers [1922]), p. 82.

12 DR. SYLVESTER GRAHAM, *Chastity, in a Course of Lectures to Young Men* (New York: Fowler and Wells, n.d.), p. 15.

13 COWAN, *Science of a New Life,* pp. 115–17.

14 JOSEPH W. HOWE, *Excessive Venery, Masturbation, and Continence* (New York: Bermingham & Company, 1883), pp. 76–77.

15 FREDERICK HOLLICK, *The Male Generative Organs in Health and Disease* (New York: T. W. Strong, n.d.), pp. 357–59.

16 TRALL, *Sexual Physiology,* pp. 247–48.

17 KELLOGG, *Plain Facts,* p. 177.

18 L. N. FOWLER, *Marriage: Its History and Ceremonies; With a Phrenological and Physiological Exposition of the Functions and Qualifications for Happy Marriages* (New York: Fowlers and Wells, Publishers, 1853), pp. 151–53, 159.

19 ELIZABETH BLACKWELL, *The Laws of Life, with Special Reference to the Physical Education of Girls* (New York: George P. Putnam, 1852), pp. 143–44.

20 DR. ELIZABETH BLACKWELL, *Counsel to Parents on the Moral Education of Their Children* (New York: Brentano's Literary Emporium, 1879), pp. 24–25.

21 COWAN, *Science of a New Life,* pp. 61–63.

CHAPTER SIX

. . . and Other Forms of Exploitation

Marriage is only the most obvious place where sexual attitudes have influence; they also form part of the larger cultural lenses through which human beings perceive their universe. Assumptions similar to those captured in advice books appeared in verdicts men and women passed on social questions, on themselves, and on other peoples. In the pre–Civil War period, for instance, anti-Catholic writers like the notorious Maria Monk carved out formidable careers by alleging licentiousness among priests and nuns. Miss Monk and fellow bigots equated secrecy and power over others with sensuality, an equation that never could have been made had sexuality been held in higher esteem. After all, enemies can only be slandered if qualities imputed to them are distasteful and dangerous, as unbridled eroticism was judged to be by orthodox morality.

In addition to anti-Catholicism, there were numerous nineteenth-century examples of salacious interest in one group or another's erotic behavior. Among these were episodes in the debate over slavery. From the 1830s until 1865, a vociferous group of Northern abolitionists urged "immediate emancipation" of bondsmen. Slavery also found staunch defenders and for three decades political, intellectual, and moral ground between the extremes gradually eroded. Few, if any, abolitionist or proslavery tracts printed in these years were primarily concerned with sex; but in various passages they did reveal how entwined assessments of social phenomena were with attitudes about sex, marriage, and reproduction. Defenders of slavery frequently took the patriarchal family for a model of social stability, with the slaveholder being equivalent to a benevolent father (a novel twist to the age's worship of secure family relations). Abolitionists, for their part, stressed licentiousness among slaves and violation of black women by white males.

Erotic exploitation was not the absolute, most basic objection abolitionists made to slavery, nor was resemblance to a well-ordered family the absolute, most basic justification defenders gave of slavery. The point is simply that sexual concerns, as a significant part of every individual's cultural and psychological make-up, help construct the framework in which all issues are discussed. This is not to say that erotic drives cause historical events; yet without understanding how a particular society defined and shaped erotic drives we cannot fully understand why members of that society acted and reacted as they did, why they found certain things defensible and others indefensible.

The two following selections give a quick glimpse into nineteenth-century discourse over slavery and race, and serve as reminders that advice manuals were just one way in which Americans exhibited their feelings about sex, reproduction, and matrimony.

Reverend Philo Tower was not a prominent member of the antislavery movement, or really even a member by much more than courtesy. A Northerner, he nevertheless supported Southern slaveholding until the early 1850s. Travel, however, brought about Tower's conversion. "Being somewhat disabled by twenty years' pulpit labor," *he sojourned leisurely through the South. What he viewed was appalling enough to send him rushing into print, joining his voice to the antislavery chorus. His testimony has the special virtue of eye-witness detail; unlike most genuine abolitionists, who spoke rather abstractly of Southern sensuality, Tower's knowledge was first-hand and his rhetoric vivid. Much of what he described, although deliberately lurid, had some basis in fact; but what Tower found worth seeing, as well as his overall evaluation of Southern life, was shaped by nineteenth-century sexual propriety. We detect in his prose the same cadences of orthodox morality heard in advice literature, only his subject was New Orleans (epitome of Southern sinfulness), not marriage or autoeroticism.*

BARRACOONS OF SLAVE WOMEN

Slave-brokers' offices, or whole barracoons of beautiful slave-women are here kept in any quantity, to let to gentlemen for sleeping companions.[1] To these girls is sometimes granted the privilege, when they arrive at the age of puberty, from twelve to fourteen, if not previously engaged by the master, to look for a man such as she may fancy, and engage herself to be his bed companion. And in this relation, she remains with him for a specified sum per month, which he pays her master, the broker. . . .

As no young man ordinarily dare think of marriage until he has made a fortune to support the extravagant style of house-keeping, and gratify the expensive taste of young women, as fashion is now educating them, many are obliged to make up their minds never to marry. One of this class undertook to show us, not long since, that it was much cheaper for him to have a quadroon as above described, than to live in any other way that he could be expected to in New Orleans. He hired, at a moderate rent, two apartments in a certain part of the town; his woman did not, except occasionally, require a servant; she did the marketing, and performed all the ordinary duties of house-keeping herself; she took care of his clothes, and in every way was economical and saving in her habits—it being her interest, if her affection for him was not sufficient, to make him as much comfort and as little expense as possible, that he might become the more strongly attached to her, and have the less occasion to leave her. He said that no one thought the less of him for it here, and added, "I know it is not right, but it is much better than the way in which most young men live who depend on salaries in New York."

Parents, guardians, and friends of the north, think I beseech you, think of these social relations, of the authorities that uphold them, and never, never suffer your sons, brothers, or any young friend that you can prevent, to come to this abandoned city [New Orleans].

After begging "the kind reader not to allow an undue fastidious taste to prevent him from reading the following," *Tower went on to unravel further* "mysteries of New Orleans." *He slipped easily from describing economic and social relations to detailing interracial sexual behavior—a natural enough transition on the surface, because economic and social oppression frequently produces sexual oppression. But Tower's eye was far sharper for the latter than for the former.*

There is . . . quite a respectable number of free colored people here, some of whom are wealthy, but their money can never raise them above their caste. Here is wherein American slavery is worse than any other now existing, or that has ever existed in all the past history of the world. Neither wealth, virtue, talent, beauty, nor accomplishment, can elevate them above their caste. It is not because of their color, for they are white, and many of them whiter, more talented, better looking, and more accomplished than many of the southern white population. These free quadroons and white women, hundreds of them, are real ladies, well educated, and dress with a profusion and taste quite astonishing to a northerner. They can marry colored freemen according to law, but such an alliance would not raise them above their class. The mulatto man, besides, would not have power to protect such a wife, the same as a white man would his. In becoming the wife of the man of color, she would necessarily perpetuate her degradation; but in prostituting herself to the white, she would elevate herself, that is, in a certain grade of southern society.

Now almost all these young women of color are educated in these prejudices, and from the tenderest age, their parents fashion them for corruption. There is a species of public balls where only white men and females of color are admitted, which is known here as also in Charleston, S.C., as the fandango ball. They are very common and very numerous in the south. The husbands, fathers, and brothers of the latter are on no account received. The mothers sometimes are, and witness, with no small amount of pride, the homage addressed to their daughters by these amorous white lords. When any gentleman present is smitten by one of these southern beauties—for they are more prepossessing in appearance than southern white ladies—he goes to the mother, or in case her mother is not present, to the girl herself, to bargain for her person for a season, or for a longer term. All this passes as a matter of course, without secrecy. These monstrous unions, as previously remarked, have not even the reserve of vice, which conceals itself from shame, as virtue does from modesty. They expose themselves openly to all eyes, without any infamy or blame attaching to the men who thus demean themselves.

Bizarre as Southern customs seemed to Tower, there was more kinship with Northern conditions than he admitted. Miscegenation, color and caste, were distinctively Southern (and significant they were); yet authors like Dr. Elizabeth Blackwell commented on corruption of poor and powerless Northern women by middle-class males, a practice lacking the racial element and refinement of "fandango balls" but depressingly similar to sexual exploitation found below the Mason-Dixon line. Such parallels did not occur to the Reverend Tower, his sensibilities offended by New Orleans.

LIFE IN NEW ORLEANS

The social relations of the great mass of society in the Crescent City are singularly peculiar, and doubtless unlike any other place within the whole range of civilization. And the principles by which the intercourse in society is regulated, are strange indeed, especially to those who have been educated and taught to believe there is some meaning and worth in virtue and chastity, and that licentiousness, fornication, and adultery are crimes, if not in the sight of God, should at least be so considered in a moral point of view, as well as against the sacredness of the domestic circle and peace of society. But here these giant, horrid evils, together with the outrages of an abandoned prostitution, appear to be regarded as matters that come as much within the routine of the social relations, and the open and unrestricted indulgence of the citizens, as a general thing, as much so as any of the common civilities of life. . . .

THE CRESCENT CITY UNMASKED

The extent of licentiousness and prostitution here is truly appalling, and doubtless without a parallel, and probably double to that of any other place in the whole civilized world. The indulgence and practice is so general and common that men seldom seek to cover up their acts, or go in disguise; but in all these things keeping their mistresses or frequenting bad houses and having women coming to their rooms at night, they do it as openly, and as much before the eyes of the world, as any other act among the common civilities of the social circle. Some idea of the extent of prostitution and licentiousness which is here exhibited on every side, can be formed from the fact that three fifths at least of the dwellings and rooms in a large portion of the city are occupied by prostitutes or by one or the other class of kept mistresses. Those women who are the companions of one man, and hold that position under a pledge of confidence not to seek intercourse with others, hold themselves very much above the character of common prostitutes, and regard themselves as respectable; and as such many of them move in society with some degree of favor and consequence. The regular prostitutes of this city are composed of a crowd, nay an army of broken down females so large that they can scarcely be numbered.

One day in my tour of observation I came pat upon whole streets and squares of these localities occupied by these poor creatures. There, said I to myself, are thousands of ruined, fallen immortal beings, once fair and beautiful, of elevated moral caste, the pride and centre of some distant family and social circle: perhaps a wife or daughter, the adored of her husband and parents, the morning star, or rising sun of a noble family, now set forever.

Most Northern commentators on Southern sexual depravity explained it is a product of slavery, particularly of the master's power over his human chattel. While agreeing that there was a lack of restraint upon young white men in New Orleans, Tower attributed the Crescent City's eroticism to forces which actually operated in Northern urban areas as well—in any place where people gathered searching for gain, cut off from their families and from traditional moral guardians. New Orleans, as described by Tower, resembles a hot-house variety of speculative, aggressive Jacksonian American society, a city less remarkable for its sins than for its style.

In view of all these abominations, doubtless the main cause of so much licentiousness, and the immense number of prostitutes, of every class, grade and color that is human, is the overwhelming number of loose irresponsible men who frequent this place. Under such circumstances as men meet here, they almost lose their identity as responsible beings, having no checks around them, and under no obligation to society, consequently no pride of character, they soon become as bold and reckless in licentiousness and crime as though the pall of night perpetually shrouded their deeds. And yet men, and *some women* too, will come here, and mingle in the rounds of dissipation and pollution, who before and while at home and in other associations, would shudder at the sight, and even at the very thought of deeds they have unhappily been lured into. Such persons I daily met at the world renowned *St. Charles Hotel* and watched them with my *Argus eyes,* and saw them finally consummate the suicidal act upon their own immortal being—plunge themselves headlong into the bottom of the raging, boiling, overflowing cauldron of everlasting death. Another cause that aids in promoting these evils, is the small portion of men who have families here. Probably not one in twenty is married, and if so, leaves a family at the north, and while here entirely forgets that at home he has left a wife, who is little dreaming of the rounds of licentiousness and dissipation that constitute the almost daily track of her truant husband. To say that now and then there is a righteous Lot among them, would be saying a great deal; truth and justice however forbid us to compromise the good with the bad, but this much we are forced to say, they are "few and far between." And thus it is, from such men, together with the thousands of transient and floating population in this singular city, that makes it more than a Sodom, and causes the sins of licentiousness, adultery and prostitution, to be regarded as the proper elements of society, and perfectly consistent with a respectable and moral standing in community, and with the character of a gentleman.

Tower was neither the first nor the last commentator to perceive New Orleans as a unique city—he was just more impervious to its charms than most. He also seems to have been unaware that objections he made to life there were echoed by clerical brethren and lay advisers distressed at licentiousness in the North.

◆§ §◆

At one point in his critique of New Orleans' depravity Philo Tower referred to "southern amalgamation" *as* "the most extraordinary exhibition of degradation to which human nature can be reduced."[2] *It was possible for Tower, and many others, to display both antislavery sentiment and a sharp distate for interracial contact. Yet Tower's prejudices paled beside those of John Van Evrie, a physician who devoted a goodly amount of effort to "proving" black inferiority and to upholding slavery. Van Evrie's justifications of the South and its peculiar institution, while fully as strident as Tower's denunciations, have an odd place in proslavery literature. Van Evrie was a New Yorker, not a Southerner; and one of his boldest defenses of slavery was published after the institution had been ended. But these were not such great anomalies as they seem. Van Evrie's loyalty to slavery was as strong as any planter's and his racism has—unfortunately—a timeless element to it. Van Evrie himself had no doubt about the correctness of his beliefs, even when they were unheeded by his section and outmoded by events. He was, however, enough a child of orthodox morality to be disturbed by abolitionist charges that slavery bred licentiousness. Particularly upset by those who claimed there was no proper marriage among slaves, he devoted a chapter to the subject in one of his works.*

Nothing, perhaps, is so repugnant to the northern mind as the notion that marriage does not exist among the "slaves" of the South, and the Abolition lecturers have given this subject the most prominent place in their terrible bill of indictment against their southern brethren.[3] The spectacle, or the seeming spectacle, of four millions of human beings living without marriage, without family, without children, with nothing but offspring, shut out, like the brutes that perish, from all the household charities, and doomed to live in universal concubinage, as it has been termed, was, to the northern and European mind, such a stupendous outrage on "humanity," that we need not wonder at their fierce indignation, or at the wild and unsparing denunciation heaped upon the authors of such boundless and unparalleled iniquity. Especially were northern women shocked and indignant, and above all others, the women of New England were excited at times to a "Divine fury" when contemplating this mighty "wickedness." . . . To women thus educated [as New Englanders are], with the utmost abhorrence of any violation of marital obligations, the seeming universal disregard of this relation, and the duties embraced in it, among the "slaves" of the South, was probably the most transcendent wrong that the mind could conceive of, and the "anti-slavery" delusion of the North has doubtless been increased to a considerable extent by this strictness or severity of female education. And if the facts were what they suppose, then indeed would their indignation and abhorrence be just enough, but strange that they should never have doubted or mistrusted these facts. Many of the most intelligent have known their sisters of the South, known them to be as virtuous, refined and womanly as themselves, and yet living every day of their lives in the shadow of this mighty wrong, and in the midst of this suppositious iniquity. Could that be possible? Could woman retain her purity, her womanly delicacy, or expand into the full stature of a true womanhood with such surroundings, in an atmosphere thus corrupt and corrupting, in a social condition where four millions of people were living without marriage, in open and utter disregard of the fundamental principle of morality as well as of social order? No, indeed, it could not be possible, and, as remarked, it is strange that the women of the North have not had misgivings of this kind, or have not mistrusted the assumed *facts* of "negro slavery" in this respect.

Van Evrie had conceded much to abolitionists: he, no less than they and other proper nineteenth-century Americans, professed allegiance to female purity and to sanctity of the family. Yet Van Evrie adamantly refused to grant that family life and sexual morality might be made tenuous by a system denying recognition to marriage among slaves.

Marriage is a natural relation that springs spontaneously from the necessities of human existence, and though a civil contract, it has a deeper and holier significance than the mere external ceremony or pledge which is thus given to the world as well as to each other.

Marriage, is of course, a natural relation among negroes as well as ourselves, and were it true that these four millions of people were living without it, then the denunciations heaped upon the people of the South would doubtless be merited. But a moment's reflection should be sufficient to convince any one, at all events any American, that with a different nature, with different faculties, different wants, and different duties of these people, there must follow a different form or modification of this relation. The negro is substantially a child or undeveloped and undevelopable man, with affections, moral wants and faculties approximating, of course, to our own, but yet so different that his happiness as well as that of the white man demands a corresponding development. The affection of the sexes strongly resembles that of our school-children. It is sudden, capricious, superficial, and temporary, and sometimes violent, but rarely permanent, or would be rarely permanent were it not for the example of the whites, whose habitudes in these respects the imitative instincts of the negro impel him to copy after. In their native Africa, and without the influence and example of the superior race, polygamy is universal. . . . Nevertheless, the natural law and the natural tendency of this people is to a single union, and probably a large majority of the native Africans have only one wife. There is no natural tendency to polygamy in any race, for the numbers of the sexes being equal, the natural impulse is to a single union. But their feeble and capricious affections lead to polygamy, and their incapacity to purchase or support wives is the only limit to the negro practice in these respects. Under the teachings and restraints of the superior race at the South, the negroes, male and female, are vastly elevated in this regard, as well as others [,] above their African habitudes. They form sexual unions or marry essentially like the whites. The parties become intimate, an affection springs up, they ask and receive the consent of their masters, and they are married by a white clergyman or by a minister of their own people. Thus far, marriage among "slaves" is, on the surface at least, an exact copy of the marriage of whites. They ask the consent of their masters, as white persons ask the consent of their parents or guardians, and they are married with the same ceremonies. . . . But here they diverge. The negro does not and can not constitute a part or portion of that mighty fabric we term society. He has no social interests, no property to guard or to devise, for though he receives and enjoys a larger portion of the proceeds of his labor than any mere laborer in Europe, everything legally belongs to the master. There are no family interests for which to provide, no reputation or character to protect, no social duties to perform, or rights to defend in his case; in short, he has no connection whatever with that vast and complicated machinery which we call society. Marriage, therefore, from our stand-point—that legal formula and social pledge so vital to the very existence of social order—is obviously absurd and impossible in the case of negroes. The natural affinity, the union of affection, the perfect adaptation so essential to a true marriage in our race, is substantially imitated and substantially similar in the case of negroes at the South, but to seek to force the negro beyond this—to force upon him the social responsibilities that attach to white people; or, in other words, to make marriage a legal contract in the case of negroes, would be as absurd as to force him to vote at an election, or to perform any other high social duties, and which are evidently impossible. In regard to his own wants, the well-being of his offspring, everything connected with the best welfare and highest happiness that his race is capable of, he now enjoys, and any attempt to force him to marry as white people marry—that is, to make marriage a civil or legal contract—is not merely impossible, but it would be a crime and a monstrous outrage upon the nature God has given him. . . . The ignorant "anti-slavery" lecturer at the North has distressing tales to tell of cruel masters who separate wives and husbands, and break up families; but while such things have doubtless happened, it is quite certain that masters have interfered a hundred times to keep them together to one instance to the contrary, or to sell them apart. Such things happen occasionally, when estates are to be settled and property divided; but the instincts of the whites and the happiness of the whites are more disturbed by them than the negroes themselves. The limited intellectual power—the feeble moral nature, and superficial and capricious affections of the negro lead him to regard these separations of wives and husbands—of parents and children, with indifference, or rather we should say he has none of our perceptions or our instincts in respect to these family relations, and therefore when they do happen he is relatively or comparatively unconscious of suffering. In his native Africa he sells his wife and children without hesitation, and all the suffering he now feels is borrowed or imitated from the whites—a feeling scarcely perceptible in his native state, but in his better and higher life at the South, it is doubtless exalted into something like a sentiment of family.

Van Evrie, in common with most polemicists, wanted to have things both ways. Although arguing that blacks imitated white family patterns and were not innately polygamous, he could not resist measuring the supposed depravity of blacks by contrasting their family relations to those of whites. One of the constants in this tortuous argument was the prevalent nineteenth-century assumption that families were the vital center of a stable moral universe.

White husbands and wives, when one dies in early life, often remain unmarried, faithful to a memory forever; and still more frequently, perhaps, the affections that bound them together in their youth remain bright and untarnished in age and to the borders of the grave. Such a thing never happened with a negro. Not one of the countless millions that have lived upon the earth was ever kept from marrying a second time by a sentiment or a memory. With their limited moral endowment such a thing is an absolute moral impossibility. They live with each other to extreme old age, because they imitate the superior race, and because it has become a habit, perhaps, but the grand purposes of nature accomplished, there is little or nothing more, or of those blessed memories of joy and suffering—of early hope and chastened sorrows, which so bind and blend together the white husband and wife, and often render them quite as necessary to each other's happiness as in the flush and vigor of youth. Affection for his master is, in fact, the strongest, and it may be said to be the only enduring affection of the negro nature, for it remains an ever-present feeling long after the feeble and capricious "family sentiment," or love of wife and offspring, is entirely obliterated from his memory.

Slavery's fate was decided by fire and Van Evrie's cause was found wanting. There was no such decisive event—no Civil War—waged over orthodox morality, largely because at that time few cared to dispute it. Although nineteenth-century sexual radicals existed, they were small in number and scantily heeded; more typically, people who disagreed violently over other issues held similar views regarding the way society should organize reproductive activity. Despite a nineteenth-century lack of consensus on political or economic questions, there was something approaching unanimity (at least among the articulate) on moral matters; and that particular consensus helped set the terms within which all social commentary took place. In the case of Tower and Van Evrie, each man imagined a radically different kind of ideal society, but each could only conceive of his particular ideal as revolving around well-ordered families, with wedlock binding the sexes and sexuality. Examples could be multiplied a hundredfold and the result would remain much the same. Abolitionists and antiabolitionists, reformers and antireformers, polemicists and counterpolemicists, all eyed opponents warily (often myopically) and failed to realize that the moral ground they did not dispute was as significant as that which they contested. Only at the nineteenth century's end did Freudian theory, cultural relativism, and other developments provide prominent enough intellectual and ethical vantage points to allow respectable men and women to see that orthodox morality itself was a fit subject for analysis, a matter to be weighed with as much logic and passion, science and pseudo-science, as Americans had previously applied to slavery and to sins even less gigantic.

1 REVEREND PHILO TOWER, *Slavery Unmasked: Being a Truthful Narrative of a Three Years' Residence and Journeying in Eleven Southern States: To Which is Added the Invasion of Kansas, Including the Last Chapter of*

Her Wrongs (New York: E. Darrow & Brother, 1856), pp. 316, 320–21, 325–27, 333, 337–41.

2 Ibid., p. 322.

3 John Van Evrie, *White Supremacy and Negro Subordination; Or, Negroes a Subordinate Race, and (So-Called) Slavery Its Normal Condition* (New York: Van Evrie, Horton & Co., 1868). Selections following are from pp. 233–234, 238–243.

CHAPTER SEVEN

Controls and Cures

Sexual morality inevitably inspired its own kinds of crusades, impelling men and women to seek to curb both social and private sins. Some tried legislation: against prostitution, for licensed prostitution, for easier divorce in cases of moral turpitude, against contraception. This legalistic approach won its grandest triumphs after 1870, in measures promoted by Anthony Comstock and fellow smut-hunters (who were hoping to prevent creation and distribution of "obscene" materials). Although Comstockery has fallen into bad repute, it is not especially remarkable that Americans turned governmental power against certain forms of erotic behavior. There were ample precedents because, from the very beginning, colonies and states had punished sexual transgressions; and, given the firmness of nineteenth-century moral prescriptions, it would be more surprising had Americans not tried to legislate morality.

Statutory prudery of Comstock's sort was less singular than was a parallel course pursued by his contemporaries—the writers of advice manuals who devised imaginative ways to help individuals restrain their own erotic impulses and cure their own sexual problems. While endorsing public action, such authors primarily sought to enlighten readers about sexuality's dangers and, having done that, to assist them in gaining mastery over private impulses.

Although advice literature began to place a new stress on sexual control after 1830, it owed a debt to earlier authorities. In 1812 Benja-

min Rush had diagnosed sexuality in much the same way his successors would—as a potentially destructive impulse. Similarly, Rush foreshadowed post-1830 writers in the means he listed to prevent erotic excess.

The remedies for [sexual] appetite, when inordinate, are natural, physical and mental.[1] They are,

1. Matrimony; but where this is not practicable, the society of chaste and modest women. . . .

2. A diet, consisting simply of vegetables, and prepared without any of the usual condiments that are taken with them. Dr. Stark found his venereal desires nearly extinguished by living upon bread and water. They revived upon a diet of bread and milk, and became more active by eating six or eight ounces of roasted goose every day, with a proportionable quantity of bread. Persons afflicted with this disease should use but little salt in their aliment. . . . In recommending a vegetable diet for the cure of this disease [excessive sexual desire], I would remark, that it is effectual only when it *succeeds* a full animal diet; for we read not only of individuals, but of whole nations, that live upon vegetables and other simple food, in whom the sexual appetite exists in its usual and natural force. In such persons the appetite should be weakened, by reducing the *quantity* of their aliment.

3. Temperance in drinking, or rather the total abstinence from all fermented and distilled liquors.

4. Constant employment in bodily labour or exercise. They both lessen venereal excitability and promote healthy excitement. Hippocrates tells us the Sythians, who nearly lived upon horseback, were free from venereal desires. Long journeys on horseback should therefore be recommended for the morbid degrees of this appetite. The chase would probably serve the same purpose. The connection between this exercise and chastity is happily illustrated by the poets in the character of Diana, who lived by hunting. The Indians owe the weakness of their venereal desires to this, among other invigorating employments.

5. The cold bath. There is a debility of body which is connected with venereal excitability, and which the cold bath is calculated to remove. This excitability is most apt to occur during the convalescence, or soon after the recovery from malignant or chronic fevers. Twelve marriages took place of the patients who recovered from the yellow fever at Bush-Hill, in the neighbourhood of this city [Philadelphia], in the year 1793; and a greater number were detected in a criminal intercourse with each other, in the private apartments and tents belonging to the hospital. I have known two instances of young clergymen, who married the women who nursed them in chronic fevers,

both of whom were in very humble life. The celebrated Mr. Howard did the same thing. These unequal matches appear to have been the effects of a morbid sexual appetite, that suddenly succeeded their fevers, and which they did not dare to gratify but in a lawful way.

6. A salivation, by diverting morbid excitability from the genitals to the mouth and throat, would probably be useful in this disease.

7. Avoiding all dalliance with the female sex. I knew a gentleman in this city, who assured me he had gained a complete victory over his venereal desires by a strict regard to this direction; and I have heard of a clergyman, who overcame this appetite by never looking directly in the face of a woman.

8. Avoiding the sight of obscene pictures, the reading [of] obscene books, and listening to obscene conversation, all of which administer fuel to the sexual appetite.

9. Certain tones of music have sometimes suddenly relieved a paroxysm of venereal desires.

10. Dr. Boerhaave says a sudden fit of laughter has sometimes had the same effect.

11. Close application of the mind to business, or study of any kind, more especially to the mathematics. Sir Isaac Newton conquered this appetite by means of the latter study, and the late Dr. Fothergill by constant application to business. Both these great and good men lived and died batchelors, and both declared, upon their death beds, that they never had known, in a single instance, a criminal connection with the female sex.

12. The influence of an active passion, that shall predominate over the sexual appetite. The love of military glory, so common among the American Indians, by combining with the hardships of a savage life, contributes very much to weaken their venereal desires.

13. Several medicines have been recommended, to subdue the excess of the sexual appetite; among these, the castor oil nut, and camphor, have been most commended. The former acts only by opening the bowels, and thereby taking off the tension of the contiguous genital organs. Any other lenient purge would probably have the same effect. If camphor have any virtues, in this disease, it must be by its stimulating powers removing that nervous debility, upon which venereal excitability depends. Any other stimulating medicine, given in a similar state of the system, would probably have the same, or a greater, effect.

I have thus mentioned all the remedies for derangement in the passions and sexual appetite. While I admit the necessity of their being aided by religious influence, in order to render them successful, I maintain that religious influence is seldom effectual for that purpose, unless it be combined with those physical remedies. This opinion is amply supported by numerous precepts in the Old and New Testaments, and it is only by inculcating those physical precepts, with such as are of a religious and moral nature, that the latter can produce their full effects upon the body and mind.

Rush, a notable early American scientist, anticipated the way advisers after him would place less faith upon divine intervention than upon physiological wisdom. Sixty-five years later even John Harvey Kellogg, a prominent Seventh Day Adventist layman, offered no support to those who preferred religion to biological law.

It would seem almost unnecessary to suggest the impropriety of resorting to prayer alone when the sexual excitability has arisen from a culpable neglect to relieve the bowels.[2] Such physical causes must be well looked after, or every attempt to reform will be fruitless. God requires of every individual to do for himself all that he is capable of doing; to employ every available means for alleviating his condition.

By making sexual control secular, nineteenth-century advisers took some responsibility off God, but only to place it upon man. Individuals could regulate erotic drives, so the message went, if they practiced rigorous self-discipline and allowed science and morality to shape personal habits. "All men can be chaste in body and in mind," *Sylvester Graham claimed,* "if they truly desire it, and if they use the right means to be so." *These means were various—although uniformly demanding. Graham placed most emphasis on proper diet. If some foods inspired sensuality then obviously other foods could be used to dampen it, a point Rush had also made. But even Graham, like most advisers, thought in terms of a complete program for restraint rather than a single cure-all.*

If an unmarried man finds himself troubled with concupiscence, let him be more abstemious, and less stimulating and heating in his diet, and take more active exercise in the open air, and use the cold bath under proper circumstances, and there will be no necessity for an emission of his semen—especially if, with proper chastity of mind, he avoid lewd images and conceptions.[3] And if a married man finds himself inclined to an excess of sexual indulgence, let him adopt the same regimen, and he will soon find that he has no reason to complain of what he calls his natural propensity.

Equally spartan were the recommendations of Dr. Augustus Gardner, given over a generation after Graham's.

The methods by which man, considered in both sexes, can diminish his venereal needs, consist in the diversion which he gives to his fancies, by devoting himself to manual labour or the culture of the sciences—in the privation which he imposes upon himself—when his sensual exigencies are especially pressing—in all that would tend to increase the tone of his organs or the excitability of the nervous system, as animal food, condiments, alcoholic drinks, coffee, &c.[4] Sleep on the back is to be avoided; long rest in bed, especially a bed too soft. Finally, the use of tepid baths, and cooling drinks of all sorts, will, as adjuvitants, be found of unquestionable utility.

Dr. John Cowan's suggestions, coming (like Gardner's) in the post–Civil War world, were particularly comprehensive, serving as a useful summary of virtually all common nineteenth-century prescriptions for sexual control. Cowan's remarks also demonstrate how little had changed since Benjamin Rush wrote in 1812.

So closely is the nature of licentiousness interwoven with that of alcoholic liquors, opium and tobacco, that it is difficult to tell which depends upon the other for its stimulus; but be that as it may, it is required as an absolute necessity that the individual give up the use of tobacco in all its forms, and ale, wine, whiskey, cider, and all other alcoholic liquors; for a man or woman cannot possibly live a chaste life, sexually or otherwise, who uses these soul-debasing articles. . . .[5]

The next notable requirement in this Plan of Life is the being moderate in eating. An almost constantly present result of licentiousness is gluttony; and when the first does not complete the work of destruction, the last invariably does. . . . Pork and fat meats at all times should be avoided, and when meat is used, it should be but once a day, and consist of lean roast beef, beefsteak or mutton. All other kinds of animal food should be ignored, as should also eggs, lobsters, crabs, oysters, and fish of all kinds, for these have a direct stimulating influence on the sexual system, and therefore should carefully be avoided by the continent man. . . .

The dress, adapted to the temperature, should be clean and comfortable; all constricting bands should be avoided, and braces always used to support the pantaloons.

By women, corsets, garters, and all articles of clothing having a tendency to interfere with the full play of the internal organs should positively be avoided.

Closely connected with food and raiment is exercise. A certain amount of physical and mental exercise and rational amusement is required every day. There is no more natural, healthy and invigorating exercise than that of walking—and by walking I do not mean the mincing, affected, formal or fashionable style of walking; but the free, loose, natural swing of the arms and legs, and the harmonious action of the body in living, happy, exhilarating, electrical motion. Persons whose occupations are of a sedentary nature should on every day of their lives take a walk of from five to ten miles. . . . Cities in which horse-cars have been introduced do much toward creating a dislike for walking. Clerks and businessmen living in such cities would do much toward the acquirement of good health if they would at all seasons avoid cars, omnibuses and carriages, for no better exercise can be secured by such men than the morning and evening walk to and from their place of business—one, two, or five miles of a walk morning, and evening, should be hailed by such as a boon greatly to be desired and appreciated.

The bedroom should be large, light and well ventilated day and night. Feather beds and pillows should be avoided. The best bed is a mattress made from straw, corn husks, curled hair, or compressed sponge. No more bed-covering should be used than is absolutely required to keep the person comfortable; it is much more desirable to be a little cool or cold in bed than to be too warm. No article of clothing should be worn at night that is worn during the day.

The individual should go to bed at a regular hour—say nine o'clock (eight o'clock would be better), and rise at five, six or seven o'clock, as is most desirable. The morning is an important period in the life of the incontinent individual, and the plan all such should adopt is to *leap out of bed as soon as they wake in the morning*. The close observance of this rule will enable the man to avoid many evil results. Thousands of men wake in the morning, having the rectum distended with hardened foeces, and pressing on the seminal receptacles behind, with the distended bladder pressing in front, and they think that the sexual part of their system is urgent for intercourse, when it is only their bowels and bladder that want evacuating. This should be well understood, for the habit of early morning licentiousness is widespread. . . .

A daily bath of the whole body is a necessity. . . .

Every-day employment should be as much of a necessity to every man (and woman) as is eating. A man who is constitutionally lazy and careless about working is nearly always a licentious man. An idle life and a chaste and continent life cannot possibly be found in the same individual; therefore it is required in the man who desires to live a continent life that he have constant employment, involving either the healthy exercise of the brain or muscular system, or both together.

The choice of companions is not lightly to be disregarded. A young man, leaving the pure associations of a happy home, and entering any of our large cities, can without much trouble form the acquaintance of a class of associates that will lead him very far from the pure, chaste, continent life he hitherto has led, and in this way the ability and genius of thousands of young men, who commence life with such bright hopes and good prospects, are fouled, blighted, and eventually destroyed in the mire of tobacco, women and wine. . . .

Especially should the continent man exercise and train his will-power, for the doing of this not only enables him to lead a continent life, but it as surely guides to success in all business undertakings. Through the right exercise of the will the body is strengthened, the soul enlarged, and right habits of thought and action increase and grow; for every victory over one's bad habits strengthens the victor. . . .

A young man, exercising a firm will and determined purpose, can surmount all obstacles that obstruct the path to a continent life.

Such cures for incontinence followed directly from nineteenth-century diagnoses of sex, its dangers and its pathology. If stimulants, bad food, and evil companions led to moral and physical destruction then, obviously, an individual could remain pure by avoiding stimulants, eating good food, and fraternizing with respectable people. But lists like Cowan's were more than mere conclusions drawn logically from prevalent beliefs about erotic impulses. Cowan and his colleagues were also exhibiting longstanding concerns, including one predating the American Revolution—a fear that luxury creates softness and decadence. Nineteenth-century middle-class prosperity gave renewed cause for alarm, particularly because it, and the conveniences of urban existence, removed men and women from rural life's chastening harshness. Even if people no longer needed to walk miles (Cowan seemed to be saying), no longer needed to sleep on rude beds in drafty rooms, and no longer had to rise at the crack of dawn, they still ought to for moral reasons. In this manner, nineteenth-century authorities tried to preserve old virtues in a changing nation, meanwhile satisfying a relatively new perception of man's biological nature.

Because life in America threatened to become too easy, it would not do merely to eat right and avoid temptations; and advisers sought effec-

tive ways to restore rigor and challenge, lest men and women wallow in sensuality and ill health. One solution gaining great favor was exercise—artificial strenuousness. Early in the century manual labor institutions offered students a chance to work as they learned, partly to support themselves and partly to improve their bodies. More practical and more common were physical education classes within conventional schools and special gymnasia catering to those in need of development or restoration. Certainly these nineteenth-century innovations had merit. Some Americans then (as now) did slide too quickly into sedentary habits, and did require more exertion than they got. But advice-manual authors also made plain their belief that exercise was essential to help subdue the passions. A sound body, they rather curiously assumed, was not a sensual body—morbid introspection, not health and vigor, encouraged licentiousness. This reasoning appears alien in a day that has fostered the term "sexercises," but it was perfectly clear in the world of authors like Dr. Frederick Hollick, where erotic drives themselves were often classified with diseases.

Now, the idle man does not expend enough vital energy on his muscular system to keep it healthy, but at the same time gives a superabundance of it to the sexual organs, so that they are over-stimulated, and suffer from excess.[6] They become habituated to great indulgence, and are constantly causing a drain on the vital power, that soon exhausts both principal and interest and leaves the individual completely exhausted. . . .

I am fully persuaded that there is no case of precocious or excessive sexual propensity, unless caused by disease, that cannot be easily subdued by *muscular exercise.* No matter how vigorously the seminal glands may act, in a state of leisure, they *must* become less active if the body be exhausted by active exertion, and to this rule there is scarcely any limit. One of the Reports of the Massachusetts Lunatic Asylum strongly impresses this truth, and shows conclusively that we have, in *hard labor,* a *certain means* of subduing this propensity to its proper limits under any circumstances. The application of this truth to young persons is obvious, numbers of whom are made licentious only by bodily inactivity and over-feeding.

Strenuous endeavors, made a part of childhood training, would surely produce adults in whom purity was second nature, as Dr. Elizabeth Blackwell argued:

The study of natural science, and of all pursuits which develop a love and observation of nature, are of great value in education.[7] Such pursuits have the additional advantage of promoting life in the open air. The weighty testimony in favor of the beneficial influence of outdoor exercises and amusements has already been noted. All experience shows us that the calling of the great muscular apparatus of the human body into constant vigorous life is an indispensable means for securing the healthy, well-balanced growth of the frame, and for preventing the premature development of the sexual faculty. It is a subject worthy of the especial study of parents, in relation to the education of both sexes. Abundant exercise in the fresh air, with total abstinence from alcoholic drink, may be considered the two great physical aids to morality in youth.

The doctrine of a vigorous life inspired many energetic late nineteenth-century Americans, including an ambitious youth named Theodore Roosevelt. Its tenets encompassed an appealing adventurousness lacking in middle-class existence, a belief that masculinity was proved in competition, and the feeling, expressed by Dr. Blackwell, that "we cannot separate the body and soul—the health of one must, as a general rule, be based upon the other."[8] *This may not have been classical theology but it sufficed in a boldly aggressive era and among people who thought vigor and purity were related.*

❧ ☙

So preoccupied were advisers with restraining sexuality that they gave far less time to curing erotic disabilities than contemporary authorities commonly do. Impotence attracted comment but frigidity received scant attention, perhaps because erotic impulses were considered to be naturally much less in females than in males, scarcely to be missed if absent. Some authorities occasionally recognized that sexual incapacity could cause mental anguish, but they did so with limited sympathy, frequently regarding impotence as just retribution for earlier excesses. This was an understandable, if sad, result of fascination with sex's presumed dangers.

Perhaps it was as well that advice-manual authors expended so little energy attempting to cure impotence. One of the small number who tried, Dr. Frederick Hollick, produced a formula that was little more than inspired quackery—although it surely would have increased a patient's happiness. Hollick's selection marks both sexual attitudes and drug laws differing from our own.

There is one drug brought from the East Indies, the *Cannabis Indica* [marijuana], which is the most regular in its action, and produces the most constant beneficial effects of anything yet tried.[9] It appears to act as a special nervous stimulant, exciting that part of the brain which influences the sexual organs, so that they feel directly an increase of power. It also causes great mental activity, disposes to cheerfulness, and induces a feeling of warmth and comfort over the whole system. Those who have taken it in a proper manner, are delighted with its effects, and never complain of any after-depression or reaction in any way. If given improperly, however, or in too heavy a dose, it first causes excitement of the wildest character, with an uncontrollable disposition to bodily activity, and afterwards a complete mental and physical prostration. In short it is most powerful, either for good or for evil, according as it is used, and is the only means we possess, in numerous cases, of restoring sexual power and desire. In the East Indies it is commonly used, like opium is in China, for the purpose of producing pleasurable excitement, and also for removing impotence.

A plant producing this drug grows in the United States, and with due care a similar preparation may be made from it to that received from the East Indies. I have experimented with both, and when prepared by myself I have found the native product fully equal to the foreign. . . .

In a particular class of cases I have long been using a combination of the Cannabis, with other articles, which I find to possess the most extraordinary powers, the preparation of which I have been repeatedly importuned to disclose, both by patients and medical men. . . . So wonderful and unexpected have been the effects of this preparation, in numerous instances, that if I chose to be unscrupulous and sell it indiscriminately, I have no doubt but it would be used more extensively than any other medicine has ever been, for any purpose whatever. . . . I do not hesitate to say that I have seen more restorations to sexual power, and more cures of *Sterility,* in both sexes, from the use of this preparation than from any other means, and I do not hesitate to pronounce it, in certain cases, *an infallible remedy.*

Dr. Hollick, a successful public lecturer, thrived in that borderland where science and showmanship join; in 1848 the Boston Post *remarked favorably on a series of talks he illustrated with a mannequin containing* "a fac simile of all the important machinery of the human body." [10] *Hollick's remedy for impotence, however, was more than an example of his sensationalism; it may well have pointed to culturally conditioned aspects of impotence and frigidity. Undoubtedly Hollick did effect "cures"; his own confidence and marijuana's power to relax inhibitions would help men and women whose sexual difficulties were primarily psychological, as is so often the case. The probable success of Hollick's formula and of sexually abstemious regimens like Sylvester Graham's*

in restoring general health raises the question of how much sexual incapacity was actually encouraged by orthodox morality, by advisers (including Hollick) who issued gloomy descriptions of damage erotic impulses could inflict. Sexual vigor had to contend with warnings that erotic activity was an imposition on women, a betrayal of man's highest nature, and potentially destructive—unless utilized in marriage for procreation, in which case it became sublimely ennobling. In face of pressures not to indulge, as well as mystical expectations about the right kind of indulgence, some men and women probably simply found asexuality the least confusing and most appealing alternative.

❧ ❧

Nineteenth-century authorities feared that people would become slaves to human erotic nature. Yet specific prescriptions for restraining, refining, and restoring sexuality hint at something else again, at a faith in mankind's ability to win the battle with eroticism. Self-discipline, diet, exercise, and other mortifications of the flesh would not have been worth advocating unless writers really believed men and women could do something about their inner urges. Rational control of sexuality, advice-manual authors implied, was both possible and the sign of truly civilized human beings. Such a line of reasoning, although easily detected in much advice literature, appeared with greatest clarity among those writers most firmly committed to the idea of social progress. For Robert Dale Owen, reform-minded son of famed reformer Robert Owen, man's capacity to guide his passions separated him from lesser creatures and gave hope for a better life to come.

Nothing so elevates man above the brute creation, as the due control of his instincts.[11] The lower animals follow them blindly, unreflectingly. The serpent gorges himself; the bull fights, even to death, with his rival of the pasture; the dog makes deadly war for a bone. They know nothing of progressive improvement. The elephant or the beaver of the nineteenth century, are just as wise, and no wiser, than the elephant or the beaver of two thousand years ago. Man alone has the power to improve, to cultivate, to elevate his nature, from generation to generation. He alone can control his instincts by reflection of consequences, and regulate his passions by the precepts of wisdom.

Dr. Elizabeth Blackwell, like Owen a veteran of antebellum reform, made virtually the same point nearly a half century later.

That the mind must possess the power of ruling this highest of the animal functions [sex], is evident from its uses, and from the nature of man.[12] The faculty of sex comes to perfection when the mind is in full activity, and when all the senses are in their freshest youthful vigor. Its object is no longer confined to the individual; it is the source of social life; it is the creator of the race. Inevitably, then, the human mind (the Emotions, the Will) must control this function more than any other function. It assumes a different aspect from all other functions through its objective character. The individual may exist without it—the race not. For this reason it is placed so largely under the control of the human Will. Necessarily, therefore, every object which addresses itself to the senses, or the mind, acts with peculiar force upon this function. Either for right or for wrong, the mind is the controlling power. The right education of the mind is the central point from which all our efforts to help the younger generation must arise.

And so the problem of controlling human eroticism came down to a matter of instilling greater knowledge and self-discipline. Although nineteenth-century advice often had a frighteningly strict and regimented appearance, it rested on a firm belief in the ability of men and women to grow in wisdom, to improve both themselves and the world around them.

Cures sometimes are worse than diseases and nineteenth-century prescriptions for sexual disorders had their own pathology, if taken to extremes. Anybody compulsively eating bland food, aggressively practicing continence, exercising furiously, and abstaining from stimulants, would—by present-day standards—be a more likely candidate for medical treatment than would an incorrigible libertine. But nineteenth-century commentaries on sexual control were not ramblings of mildly disordered minds; they represented serious attempts to reconcile a particularly suspicious view of erotic impulses with a pronounced faith in mankind's ability to control its own destiny. Advisers warned people that threats to their very existence resided within them, in their sexual urges; yet these same writers also conveyed the more subtle, more optimistic message that both responsibility and power to curb such threats likewise resided within each person. Reform of sexual disorders, even in the age of Anthony Comstock and legalized prudery, began with the individual and (so authorities proclaimed) could largely be achieved by enlightened and determined individuals.

---

1 Benjamin Rush, *Medical Inquiries and Observations, Upon the Diseases of the Mind* (Philadelphia: Kimber & Richardson, 1812), pp. 351–56.

[2] J. H. Kellogg, *Plain Facts about Sexual Life* (Battle Creek, Michigan: Office of the Health Reformer, 1877), p. 130.

[3] Dr. Sylvester Graham, *Chastity, in a Course of Lectures to Young Men* (New York: Fowler and Wells, Publishers, n.d.), p. 16.

[4] Augustus K. Gardner, *The Conjugal Relationships as Regards Personal Health and Hereditary Well-Being Practically Treated,* 5th ed. (Glasgow: Thomas D. Morison, 1905), pp. 64–65.

[5] John Cowan, *The Science of a New Life* (New York: Cowan & Company, Publishers, 1880), pp. 122–27.

[6] Frederick Hollick, *The Male Generative Organs in Health and Disease,* 120th ed. [sic.] (New York: T. W. Strong, n.d.), p. 354.

[7] Dr. Elizabeth Blackwell, *Counsel to Parents on the Moral Education of Their Children* (New York: Brentano's Literary Emporium, 1879), p. 119.

[8] Elizabeth Blackwell, *The Laws of Life, with Special Reference to the Physical Education of Girls* (New York: George P. Putnam, 1852), p. 167.

[9] Hollick, *Male Generative Organs,* pp. 303–305.

[10] Cited as a testimonial in Hollick, *Male Generative Organs,* p. 457.

[11] Robert Dale Owen, *Moral Physiology; Or, A Brief and Plain Treatise on the Population Question* (London: J. Watson, 1841), pp. 12, 13.

[12] Blackwell, *Counsel to Parents,* pp. 32–33.

CHAPTER EIGHT

The Welcome Child

The desire to control sexual impulses forced authors of nineteenth-century advice manuals to consider how (or whether) men and women ought consciously to control reproduction. Actually the impulse to thwart conception is probably as old as mankind; evidence of deliberate contraception appears in the Bible and in other sources from the ancient world.[1] *Until the end of the eighteenth century, however, birth control seems largely to have been a private matter, something practiced by individuals as best they could but without inspiring much public discussion. Thomas Robert Malthus helped change all this by anonymous publication, in 1798, of* An Essay on the Principle of Population as It Affects the Future Improvement of Society. *Malthus, a gentle and vague English clergyman, argued that human procreation tended to outrace natural resources, that population could increase far more rapidly than foodstuffs available to feed hungry mouths. Only disasters—wars, famines, and epidemics—kept mankind and its food supply in tenuous balance; but the price was misery for much of humanity, doomed to suffer the grim consequences of excessive reproduction. Malthus did not personally endorse contraception, instead urging those who sought population limitation to practice continence (or "moral restraint") and to marry fairly late in life. Yet Malthus' gloomy prognosis touched off considerable controversy in Europe and America; and, inevitably, contraception became part of the issue, no matter what Malthus thought about it. There was simply no way to argue about reproductive behavior without bringing up the possibility of artificial birth control.*

Americans were prime among Malthus' bad examples: their staggering colonial population increase was a sign of what the unfettered reproductive instinct could accomplish. Quick though Americans were to procreate, they were far slower than the British in producing birth control literature. In 1822 an Englishman named Francis Place published Illustrations and Proofs of the Principle of Population, *in which he advocated contraception rather than Malthusian restraint. Place also printed handbills designed to inform men and women (particularly British "working people") of techniques to avoid pregnancy, including both coitus interruptus and obstructive devices. Place influenced other writers to take up the cause by the mid-1820s, most notably Richard Carlile, whose* What is Love? *(later entitled* Every Woman's Book) *marked him as a blunt and intrepid proponent of contraception. Despite this English activity, it was not until 1830 that an American work, Robert Dale Owen's* Moral Physiology, *dealt favorably with birth control.*

Owen drew upon European population literature—indeed, he listed his father as a contributor to it; and he shared both Malthus' fear of unlimited procreation and Place's desire to improve working-class prosperity. But Owen also developed most of the pro–birth control arguments used by later American writers.

I pray my readers . . . distinctly to observe how the matter stands.[2] Population, unrestrained, *must* increase beyond the possibility of the earth and its produce to support. At present it *is restrained by vice and misery*. The only remedy which the orthodoxy of the English clergyman [Malthus] permits him to propose, is, late marriages. The most enlightened observers of mankind are agreed, that nothing contributes so positively and immediately to demoralize a nation, as when its youth refrain, until a late period, from forming disinterested connections with those of the other sex. The frightful increase of prostitutes, the destruction of health, the rapid spread of intemperance, the ruin of moral feelings, are, to the mass, the *certain* consequences. . . .

But this is not all. Not only is Malthus' proposition fraught with immorality, in that it discountenances to a late age those disinterested sexual connections which can alone save youth from vice; but it is *impracticable.* Men and women will scarcely pause to calculate the chances they have of affording support to the children ere they become parents: how, then, should they stop to calculate the chances of the world's being overpeopled? Mr. Malthus may say what he pleases, they never will make any such calculation; and it is folly to expect they should. . . .

I will here state an opinion from which, if I read Mr. Malthus' doctrine right, he will not dissent. I am convinced that at this moment there is nothing approaching to an *absolute* excess of population in any country of Europe. Iniquitous laws, false education, and a vicious order of things are continually producing effects which are erroneously attributed to over population. The effect springs not from the absolute number, but from the ignorance of men. . . .

Thus (and I am desirous to be distinctly understood) a solution of the population question is offered, as an *alleviation* of existing evils, not as a *cure* for them—as a palliative, not as a remedy for the national disease. Population might be but a tenth part of what it is, and unjust legislation and vicious customs would still give birth, as they now do, to extravagance and want. It is true, and ought to be remembered, that the check I propose, by diminishing the number of labourers, will render labour more scarce, and consequently of higher value in the market; and in this view, its political importance is considerable. But it may also be doubted whether our present overgrown system of commercial competition be not hurrying the labourer towards the lowest rate of wages capable of sustaining life, too rapidly to be overtaken, except in individual cases, even by a prudential check to population. . . .

The great importance of the present work I conceive to lie more in its moral and social, than in its political bearings. It is addressed to each individual rather as the member of a family than as the citizen of a state. . . .

What would be the probable effect, in social life, if mankind obtained and exercised a control over the instinct of reproduction?

My settled conviction is—and I am prepared to defend it—that the effect would be salutary, moral, civilizing; that it would prevent many crimes, and more unhappiness; that it would lessen intemperance and profligacy; that it would polish the manners and improve the moral feelings; that it would relieve the burden of the poor, and the cares of the rich; that it would most essentially benefit the rising generation, by enabling parents generally more carefully to educate, and more comfortably to provide for, their off-spring. . . .

And first, let us look solely to the situation of married persons. Is it not notorious, that the families of the married often increase beyond what a regard for the young beings coming into the world, or the happiness of those who give them birth, would dictate? In how many instances does the hard-working father, and more especially the mother of a poor family, remain slaves throughout their lives, tugging at the oar of incessant labour, toiling to live, and living only to die; when, if their offspring had been limited to two or three only, they might have enjoyed comfort and comparative affluence! How often is the health of the mother—giving birth, every year, perchance, to an infant

—happy, if it be not twins! and compelled to toil on, even at those times when nature imperiously calls for some relief from daily drudgery—how often is the mother's comfort, health, nay, her life, thus sacrificed! . . .

Yet this is not all. Every physician knows, that there are many women so constituted that they cannot give birth to healthy, sometimes not to *living* children. Is it desirable—is it *moral,* that such women should become pregnant? Yet this is continually the case, the warnings of physicians to the contrary notwithstanding. Others there are, who ought never to become parents; because, if they do, it is only to transmit to their offspring grievous hereditary diseases; perhaps that worst of diseases, insanity. Yet they will not lead a life of celibacy. They marry. They become parents; and the world suffers by it. That a human being should give birth to a child, knowing that he transmits to it hereditary disease, is in my opinion, an immorality. But it is a folly to expect that we can ever induce all such persons to live the lives of Shakers. Nor is it necessary. All that duty requires of them is to refrain from becoming parents. Who can estimate the beneficial effects which rational, moral restraint may thus have on the physical improvement of our race, throughout future ages! Were such virtue as this generally cultivated, how soon might the very seeds of disease die out amongst us, instead of bearing, as now, their poisoned fruit, from generation to generation! and how far might human beings, in succeeding times, surpass their forefathers in health, in strength, and in beauty! . . .

Is it not most plainly, clearly, incontrovertibly *desirable,* that parents *should have the power* to limit their offspring, whether they choose to exercise it or not? Who *can* lose by their having this power? and how many *may* gain—may gain competency for themselves, and the opportunity carefully to educate and provide for their children! How many may escape the jarrings, the quarrels, the disorder, the anxiety, which an overgrown family too often causes in the domestic circle!

Owen's work stirred a Massachusetts physician, Dr. Charles Knowlton, to publish anonymously, in 1832, Fruits of Philosophy. *Knowlton drew heavily upon* Moral Physiology, *and he echoed Owen's feeling that continence and late marriage were unlikely to gain popularity among young people.* "Does not wisdom bid us temperately enjoy the spring-time of life?" *he asked.*[3] *But Knowlton, an interesting figure who was a philosopher as well as a medical man, repaired something of a deficiency in Owen's book. Although pleading eloquently for birth control,* Moral Physiology *was so tastefully and carefully written and so concerned with general amelioration of mankind's lot, that it gave little specific information on contraceptive methods, despite Owen's endorsement of coitus interruptus. Knowlton, however, offered details on what he considered a new and sure technique: douching. For his trouble he was fined by scandalized authorities in Taunton, Massachusetts, and thrown in jail in Cambridge. Knowlton's advice, nevertheless, was significant enough, and apparently reliable enough, to remain in circulation in America and in England for decades. Perhaps over 40,000 copies of* Fruits of Philosophy *were distributed in Britain between 1834 and 1876, and it was to achieve even greater notoriety there after 1877, when the government prosecuted its publishers.*

❧

Moral Physiology *and* Fruits of Philosophy *were only a beginning, although an impressive one. The topic quickly passed on to other authors, some of them fashioning arguments for the same limited and high-minded readership Owen and Knowlton hoped to reach, others cruder and less scrupulous. Eventually even the popular press contributed its portion, carrying thinly veiled advertisements for compounds intended to be used as contraceptives and abortifacients. Yet few later pro–birth control publicists, at least before Margaret Sanger in the twentieth century, surpassed Owen's dignified and often sensitively impassioned justification of contraception and Knowlton's technical innovativeness. Furthermore, the terms on which men and women supported contraception were to stay rather constant throughout the rest of the century. Details, of course, varied, and not all proponents chose to accept every available favorable argument; but birth control, much as Owen believed, was said to preserve female health, increase working-class prosperity, allow early marriage (and thus keep youth from frequenting places of debauchery), and assist in improving both society and the human race.*

Despite promising such a formidable list of benefits, birth control had many cultural barriers to surmount in the United States—it was probably far easier to practice than to defend in public controversy. For one thing, distress at population growth was less natural in America than in thickly settled European countries. Americans were accustomed to regarding their increase in numbers with pride, as a symbol of rising national glory and as an omen that the United States would surpass decadent Europe in people and power. With an abundance of open land and a well-developed expansive urge, Americans might grant—as Owen did—that overpopulation was a possibility, but place it well in the misty future, too remote to worry about. As late as 1886, when Americans could scarcely avoid awareness of crowded cities and a nagging sense that the frontier was closing, overpopulation was still far from being a compelling fear, even in the mind of a staunch birth control advocate like Dr. E. B. Foote, Jr.

Malthusianism as a national question is an interesting one, involving as it does, a study of the possible rate of increase of a people living under favorable conditions, their power to make the earth yield products for their sustenance, and the possibility, in the course of time, of a population too great in numbers to be assured a sufficiency of food products.[4] This phase of the question the writer is content to leave to future generations, hoping that long before it shall have become a live issue in America, other more pressing national questions relating to labor and the distribution of the products of labor will have been satisfactorily solved, so that it may be possible for the United States to give practical proof of how large a population (how many inhabitants to the acre) this land can comfortably support, as it has already proved during one hundred years of existence that Malthus' ratio of a population doubling itself every twenty-five years is possible. It is sufficient for my purpose here and now to show, as has just been done, how over-population, or as it is better called under such circumstances, excessive child-bearing, operates to the detriment of comfort, the sacrifice of health, over-work, overcrowding, puny off-spring, squalor and pauperism with their attendant vices, crimes and miseries, and necessarily results in a great waste of health and wealth.

In addition to having little concern for overpopulation, nineteenth-century Americans held other attitudes which formed at least potential impediments to birth control publicists. Among these was a high regard for children. The child appeared as subject of much maudlin attention in the day's literature, painted in pastel hues as an angel of innocence and joy. To youth belonged future glory and powers of redemption from adult depravity—in stories, dramas, and polemics mere babes led their elders into sobriety and renunciation of sin. Authors like Dr. John Cowan were able to turn these sentiments into an argument against contraception and other forms of conscious family limitation.

A married life without children is an unlovable and unsatisfactory life.[5] It is incomplete. It lacks the bands that make perfect the love-union between man and wife—the new birth, that makes the twain as one in flesh and spirit. But this incompleteness continues, is widened and confirmed, when the new birth is undesired by either party.

Men and women do not reach their true status in this world—do not fulfill their mission to populate—do not attain the full royalty of their natures, until they originate and rear a child; and in proportion to the number of children they rear is the royalty of their souls perfected.

Cowan made avoiding procreation seem almost inhuman, but his line of reasoning was too ambiguous to be the most effective advanced against birth control. Cowan himself claimed that the beauties of child-raising were only present when parents desired offspring, a damaging admission which could cut both ways—for contraception as well as against it. Cowan concluded that children were so desirable that people should have several; birth control advocates, on the other hand, agreed that children were precious, but insisted they were best enjoyed in small numbers, produced by parents whose health and fortunes were not exhausted by large families. This latter argument, made as early as Moral Physiology, *neatly turned the tables on writers like Cowan who sought to enlist sentimentality against contraception.*

Birth control advocates faced far greater obstacles than American regard for children and apathy toward the prospect of overpopulation. Orthodox morality itself posed what were perhaps the most formidable barriers of all in its definitions of sexuality and proper sexual behavior. By presenting erotic expression as something dangerous, to be strictly rationed, most nineteenth-century authorities left nonprocreative sex scant room. "A very few hold that the sexual act should never be indulged except for the purpose of reproduction," *wrote John Harvey Kellogg about his colleagues,* "and then only at periods when reproduction will be possible. Others, while equally opposed to . . . excesses . . . limit indulgence to the number of months in the year." [6] *Although Kellogg's summary omitted some who were more lenient, it was reasonably accurate. Men and women holding such opinions could not be expected to endorse contraception, which plainly meant sex without reproduction and therefore seemed an invitation to indulgences Kellogg and like-minded writers hoped to stamp out. The conclusion was foregone. Birth control signified, to Kellogg's ilk, nothing more than sensuality, an evasion of sex's one legitimate function. Dr. Cowan put these moral objections to contraception as explicitly and unsympathetically as anyone:*

One of the sequences to licentiousness is a desire to prevent undesirable results in the wife or betrayed woman.[7] By those married, the reasons given for the wish to avoid child-bearing are many, and a few of them may be entitled to some weight. Thus, a married woman having a small pelvis has a just dread of child-bearing. A mistake occurs in such a woman marrying at all, or at least to a man much larger in stature than herself. Again, through constitutional or local disease, she cannot become pregnant without endangering her life. Another of the reasons why conception should not take place, is through a desire to prevent the entailment of hereditary disease. People so situated, rather than seek means to prevent ill results, should be placed in such relations to life as would restore them to sound health.

The prime reason for the desire for knowledge on this subject is that licentiousness may have full play without restriction; and it will be found, in the great majority of married lives, that it is the wife who desires this knowledge, so as to guard her health, aye, her very life, against the unbridled passion of the husband. The pains, the troubles, the heart-burnings, the sickness, the danger of premature death, the woman has to experience through man's lust is beyond all comprehension, and if there is one direction more than another in which "Woman's Rights" should assert itself, it is in this one of choice of time for sexual congress.

Cowan and moralists like him objected to any nonreproductive sexual activity; but their association of contraception with depravity was reinforced by the obvious desire of libertines and prostitutes to avoid pregnancies, and by open advocacy of contraception among scandalous visionaries such as John Humphrey Noyes. Noyes, and some few other utopians, made population control part of schemes for social salvation, and did so in ways antithetical to conventional morality. Noyes' Oneida Community practiced "complex marriage," *which permitted sexual relationships to form and dissolve, governed by mutual consent and community approval; and a necessary part of* "complex marriage" *was* "male continence," *or intercourse without ejaculation.* "This abominable practice," *John Harvey Kellogg wrote scornfully,* "can be considered as nothing better than double masturbation." [8]

Yet opponents of birth control badly misunderstood their adversaries when branding them promoters of licentiousness. Respectable supporters of contraception from Owen onward vigorously upheld chastity and sexual self-control, going no farther than to defend limited intercourse among married couples and to maintain that children should not be borne at the risk of health and happiness. Less respectable supporters, including Noyes himself, likewise generally refused to condone unfettered eroticism. Birth control was, for them, usually part of a program of "higher" purity in which sexual expressiveness was presumed to gain meaning when it became a matter of consent and joy rather than of legal sanction and uncertain consequences. Noyes' own defense of "male continence" spoke in terms of sexual restraint quite similar to those employed by orthodox moralists—it would be difficult to imagine a more chaste rationale for unconventional sexual practices than that announced by Noyes.

[We at Oneida] have found licentious persons almost uniformly opposing that doctrine [male continence] with bitterness and scorn.[9] The real self-denial which it requires cannot be adjusted to their schemes of pleasure-seeking. And in any case the actual use of it by such persons could only improve their morals and mitigate the evils of their misdoings. . . .

We are not opposed, after the Shaker fashion, or even after [Robert Dale] Owen's fashion, to the increase of population. We believe that the order to "multiply" attached to the race in its original integrity, and that propagation, rightly conducted and kept within such limits as life can fairly afford, is a blessing second only to sexual love. But we are opposed to *involuntary* procreation. A very large proportion of all children born under the present system are begotten contrary to the wishes of both parents, and lie nine months in their mother's womb under their mother's curse or a feeling little better than a curse. Such children cannot be well organized. We are opposed to *excessive,* and of course oppressive procreation, which is almost universal. We are opposed to *random* procreation, which is unavoidable in the marriage system. But we are in favor of *intelligent, well-ordered* procreation. The physiologists say that the race cannot be raised from ruin till propagation is made a matter of science; but they point out no way of making it so. Propagation is controlled and reduced to a science in the case of valuable domestic brutes; but marriage and fashion forbid any such system among human beings. We believe the time will come when involuntary and random propagation will cease, and when scientific combination will be applied to human generation as freely and successfully as it is to that of other animals. The way will be open for this when amativeness can have its proper gratification without drawing after it procreation, as a necessary sequence.

Noyes went on to dismiss possible medical objections to "male continence" and its suppression of ejaculation.

It is seriously believed by many that nature requires a periodical and somewhat frequent discharge of the seed, and that the retention of it is liable to be injurious. Even if this were true, it would be no argument against Male Continence, but rather an argument in favor of masturbation; for it is obvious that before marriage men have no lawful method of discharge but masturbation; and after marriage it is as foolish and cruel to expend one's seed on a wife merely for the sake of getting rid of it, as it would be to fire a gun at one's best friend merely for the sake of unloading it. If a blunderbuss must be emptied, and the charge cannot be drawn, it is better to fire into the air than to kill somebody with it. But it is not true that the seed is an excrement like the urine, that requires periodical and frequent discharge. . . .

Closely connected with this popular fallacy respecting the seed, is the suggestion of certain medical men that the practice of Male Continence would lead to seminal degeneracy and impotence. The experience of the Community has signally refuted this suggestion in the only effectual way, viz., by a great number of intentional impregnations, which have occurred, within a few years between persons who have been longest in the practice of Male Continence.

Another apprehension suggested by medical men has been, that the avoidance of the crisis in sexual intercourse would so increase and prolong the excitement as to induce excesses, which would lead to various nervous diseases. . . . [A] professional examination [of Oneida] was instituted and a report made by Theodore R. Noyes, M.D., in which it was shown, by careful comparison of our statistics with those of the U.S. census and other public documents, that the rate of nervous diseases in the Community is considerably below the average in ordinary society.

Having made clear the need for birth control and demonstrated the physiological soundness of "male continence," Noyes warned of its moral rigor—and put in a word for erotic restraint.

Male Continence in its essence is self-control, and that is a virtue of universal importance. To cultivate self-control in respect to the seminal crisis, but neglect it in other sexual indulgences, is evidently Male Continence in a spurious and dangerous form. It is certain that this spurious self-control may be cultivated even for the purpose of gaining freedom for sensual and riotous pleasure. We may be thankful that such a counterfeit cannot escape the checks prepared for universal vice. Nothing less than heart-abandonment to the grace of God, which teaches and gives *temperance in all things,* can ever release us from the old tutelage of suffering. Our theory in its oldest form defined the sexual organs as conveyancers, not only of the seed, but of the "social magnetism." Now it is certain that the social magnetism is a vital element, as real as the seed, and as really limited in its supply; and that the loss of it in excessive quantities entails diseases as atrocious as those which follow seminal waste.

It is doubtful that John Humphrey Noyes, utopian, and John Harvey Kellogg, strait-laced medical entrepreneur, would have acknowledged any common ground at all. But both men—notorious proponent of contraception no less than his rigidly moral opponent—were seekers after demanding kinds of sexual control. Noyes' variety made intercourse subject to tightly prescribed patterns while Kellogg's nearly eliminated it altogether. Still, as so often happens in vehement discussions of social issues, the disputants accepted far more assumptions than they disagreed upon. Whatever else nineteenth-century birth control was, its advocates (whether a scandalous Noyes or a chaste Owen) did not intend it as an absolute freeing of eroticism, nor did they regard it as an assault on childbearing and other sacred tenets of orthodox morality.

If it was easy for nineteenth-century anticontraceptive and procontraceptive polemicists to misconstrue each other's beliefs, it is even easier—from a twentieth-century perspective—to dismiss them both. Although the debate itself still goes on, the terms have changed markedly. Present-day writers do defend birth control, as Owen did, by claiming it will free women from unwanted pregnancies and raise working people's standard of living; and other contemporary writers do charge, as Owen's opponents did, that birth control leads inevitably to licentiousness. But Malthus' great fear—overpopulation—has become a real issue, as it was not in the nineteenth century; and both sides today accept sexual expressiveness far less reluctantly than did their counterparts of the past. Furthermore, the physiological basis for contraceptive and anticontraceptive arguments has changed. No longer is erotic excess presented as much of a threat, and the mechanics of reproduction are better understood and more skillfully circumvented.

Time, however, has worked most unkindly on anticontraceptive arguments. Although birth control has not completely won the day, it is publicly professed and privately practiced among a great number of respectable people; and its nineteenth-century proponents (the ones of Robert Dale Owen's calibre) presently command respect for their high-minded courage and pioneering zeal, if nothing else. Anticontraceptive writers, on the other hand, seem fretful, sometimes silly, and—worse—destructive. They took an especially narrow view of erotic activity; they were remarkably insensitive to the plight of women who could not bear children or did not wish to; and they had little sympathy for the working poor, overburdened with progeny they could not support. Yet there was a case to be made against birth control for those who took nineteenth-century moral and medical orthodoxy seriously; and it was not a contemptible case, even though it may often appear, by present-day reasoning, wrong-headed. Opponents of birth control, just like supporters, found contemporary science and concern for suffering humanity to be on their side. Dr. Augustus Gardner wrapped himself in both mantles as he discussed "Methods Used to Prevent Conception, and Their Consequences."

The means used for preventing conception, more particularly affecting women, together with the more bodily injurious, more nervously exhausting and more sinfully demoralising procedures, for the purpose of destroying and making away with the results of conception—these are the crying evils of the age and of the world. . . .[10]

Let us see now what are the consequences to those given to this practice of conjugal onanism [contraception].

In man the genesiac act, accomplished normally and completely, leaves at its close a condition of well-being comparable to that which results from the satisfaction of an imperious necessity. To the most formidable nervous disturbance soon succeeds a perfect calm, and from the most troubled disposition of mind a tendency to gaiety and warmth of heart. On the contrary, when the function has been interrupted by a previous calculation, the erethism persists, accompanied by prostration and fatigue, and particularly a tinge of sadness, in which we are tempted to see a phenomenon of conscience akin to remorse—the first chastisement for a fault committed. . . .

If the good harmony of families, and the reciprocal relations are seriously menaced by the invasion of these detestable practices, the health of women, as we have already intimated, is fearfully injured. A great number of neuralgias appear to us to have no other cause. Many women that we have interrogated on this matter, have fortified this opinion. But that which to us has passed to the condition of incontestable truth, is the prevalence of uterine troubles of evervation among the married, hysterical symptoms which are met with in the conjugal relation as often as among young virgins, arising from the vicious habits of the husbands in their conjugal intercourse. We recommend this etiological point to the investigations and meditations of physicians.

Still more, there is a graver affection, which is daily increasing, and which, if nothing arrests its invasion, will soon have attained the proportions of a scourge; we speak of the degeneration of the womb. We do not hesitate to place in the foremost rank, among the causes of this redoubtable disease, the refinements of civilization, and especially the artifices introduced in our day in the genesiac act. When there is no procreation, although the procreative faculties are excited, we see these pseudo-morphoses arise. . . .

It is undeniable that all the methods employed to prevent pregnancy are physically injurious. Some of these have been characterised with sufficient explicitness, and the injury resulting from incomplete coitus to both parties has been made evident to all who are willing to be convinced. It should require but a moment's consideration to convince anyone of the harmfulness of the common use of cold ablutions and astringent infusions and variously medicated washes. . . .

When in the general state of nervous and physical excitement attendant upon coitus, when the organs principally engaged in this act, are congested and turgid with blood, do you think you can with impunity throw a flood of cold, or even luke-warm water far into the vitals in a continual stream? Often, too, women add strong medicinal agents, intended to destroy by dissolution, the spermatic germs, ere they have time to fulfil their natural destiny. These powerful astringents suddenly corrugate and close the glandular structure of the parts, and this is followed necessarily by a corresponding reaction, and the final result is debility and exhaustion, signalised by leucorrhoea, proiapsus, and other diseases.

Finally, of the use of intermediate tegumentary coverings made of thin rubber or gold-beater's skin, and so often relied upon as absolute preventives, Madame de Stael is reputed to have said: "They are cobwebs for protection, and bulwarks against love." Their employment certainly must produce a feeling of shame and disgust utterly destructive of the true delight of pure hearts and refined sensibilities. They are suggestive of licentiousness and the brothel, and their employment degrades to bestiality the true feelings of manhood and the holy state of matrimony. Neither do they give, except in a very limited degree, the protection desired. Furthermore, they produce (as alleged by the best modern French writers, who are more familiar with the effects of their use than we in the United States) certain physical lesions from their irritating presence as foreign bodies, and also from the chemicals employed in their fabrication and other effects inseparable from their employment, ofttimes of a really serious nature.

I will not further enlarge upon these instrumentalities. Sufficient has been said to convince anyone that to trifle with the grand functions of our organism, to attempt to deceive and thwart nature in her highly ordained prerogatives—no matter how simple seem to be the means employed—is to incur a heavy responsibility and run a fearful risk. It matters little whether a railroad train is thrown from the track by a frozen drop of rain or a huge boulder lying in the way, the result is the same, the injuries as great. Moral degradation, physical disability, premature exhaustion and decrepitude are the result of these physical frauds, and force upon our convictions the adage which the history of every day confirms, that *Honesty is the best policy*.

Modern authorities are less convinced than Dr. Gardner that contraception is a "physical fraud," *but he was not entirely mistaken. Methods of birth control available in his day were unreliable and unsatisfactory; and, while generally not causing maladies he attributed to them, they did pose mental and biological dangers. Coitus interruptus, by the psychological stress it places upon both parties, could have been partly responsible for some of the nervous disorders Gardner blamed on birth control. Use of unsanitary devices and of impure or harsh douches undoubtedly brought about injuries of the sort Gardner professed to see. Gardner's fault was in thinking the occasional bad consequences he glimpsed were inevitable, and in failing to realize it could be as much an imposition on human beings to conceive children as to avoid conception.*

Nineteenth-century opponents of birth control would undoubtedly generate more contemporary sympathy had they been content to rely upon science and morality to uphold their position. Instead, they called upon law for additional support. Among achievements claimed by post–Civil War enemies of licentiousness was the "Comstock Law" of 1873. Named in honor of Anthony Comstock, most tenacious of the vice-hunters, this was a federal statute banning distribution of contraceptive literature through the mails. Lest anything slip past the Comstock Law's sieve, various states also had their own anticontraceptive legislation. In addition to making discussion more difficult, such statutes seemed deliberate attempts to deprive men and women of moral choice, to foreclose consideration of the issue.

Compulsion may mark weakness—inability to command allegiance any other way. Certainly a declining American birth rate indicated that by 1873 anticontraceptive forces might be losing the battle in the field, no matter how they were doing in legislatures and courts. Yet the Comstock Law had its victims, among them Edward Bliss Foote, a physician who had for some years advocated contraception in popular works of medical advice. Baited into sending a birth control pamphlet through the mails, Foote was prosecuted in 1876 and eventually fined $3,000, with an even larger amount left to pay in costs. Foote, unrepentant, continued to promote birth control, as did his son, Edward Bliss Foote, Jr. The younger Foote, undoubtedly with his father's tribulations in mind, published in 1886 a lively attack upon the efforts of Comstock and his allies, an assault which had both personal engagement and the virtue of summarizing many points still contested more than half a century after Robert Dale Owen brought the question of contraception into print.

Let us consider the physiological and moral objections to contraception, and on this field the skirmish (for it is hardly a close battle as yet), is at present, and has been for some time, a triangular contest between three parties:[11]

1st. Those arrayed under the flag of the Alpha, declaring for celibacy before marriage, and "marital continence" in marriage, with no exception "except for purpose of reproduction."

2nd. Those who admit that under some circumstances (with a large variety of opinion with reference to the circumstances) it is proper, wise and expedient to advise or make use of contraceptics, but that they should not be generally accessible.

3rd. Those who believe that the science and art of contraception should be studied, developed and improved, and that what is now known or hereafter to be discovered should be published, as is all science, without fear or favor.

Doing battle, as I shall, from the third standpoint, let me level my guns first upon the small but sturdy guard of the Alpha flag, not with any expectation of routing them, or any desire to spike their guns, for we agree with them in some points as thoroughly as we disagree in others, and our battle with them is mainly to maintain our own position and show that we are right in holding it. The first party claim to hold the most advanced ground "founded upon religion, science and the highest and purest morality and philanthropy," and into the camp of the third party they throw this hot shot, viz.: That any exercise of the sexual function except for procreation, is "immoral, unnatural and injurious." This the third party repels and denies, while loading and firing in return the historical fact that the most strenuous religious, moral and governmental efforts to enforce celibacy and continence have been not only unsuccessful, but inevitably and proportionately attended with physical degeneracy and moral debasement, and notably with an increase of prostitution. . . .

Were it true, as claimed by ultra-moralists that there ought, in the perfect state, to be no indulgence of the sexual passion except for procreation, and that only under such conditions as would favor the best quality of offspring, it is at once apparent that this standard is so far beyond the existing practice and belief that it can be adopted in but comparatively rare instances as a working formula, and while we are awaiting the approach of the millennial day when it will be universally welcomed, we might avail ourselves of something a little less divine and perfect, by which to give humanity a lift out of the present slough of imperfection. For the present and some centuries to come, we may as well depend upon contraception as a lesser evil to help us up toward the greater good, if so it be, of strict continence. . . .

IS CONTRACEPTION PHYSICALLY INJURIOUS?

To make any satisfactory reply to the Alphites upon this important question, it would be necessary to go minutely into the discussion of ways and means, to compare freely the various methods of contraception which have been adopted or proposed, and to carefully weigh all the objections offered on physiological grounds against these several methods; but not being ready to enter upon this practical department of the subject, we will be content here with merely stating the opinion of many competent physicians who have had good opportunities for studying the merits and demerits of many contraceptic methods, viz.: The opinion that while there are more bad than good ones, yet there are means which are entitled to be considered as fairly reliable and harmless—in fact, physiologically unobjectionable.

COMSTOCK, COLGATE & CO. (LIMITED)

Having given sufficient attention to the Alphites, for present purposes, I pass on to a consideration of the position of the second party, those who recognize the utility of contraceptics, while at the same time assuming to discover in them a dangerous element which makes it seem to them wise and expedient to hedge them about with prohibitory laws; laws which were enacted by their request, and whose enforcement has thus far been left to their judgment or discretion, if we can really attribute such qualities to them.

In this camp Foote placed Anthony Comstock, his father's old adversary, and Comstock's Society for the Suppression of Vice. After mentioning Comstock's triumphs in securing anticontraceptive legislation, Foote pointed out what he regarded as fallacies in such statutes—and found examples of hypocrisy in Comstock and his supporters, particularly in Samuel Colgate.

One would naturally suppose that an association of men who should urge and put through laws shutting down entirely on the manufacture and sale of contraceptics, must be thoroughly convinced that there could be no legitimate use for them, or, that having what might be called a compromise opinion in regard to them, that they would have included in their framing of a new law some excepting clause which would have made it possible for them to be sold under certain restrictions, as for instance by the advice or prescription of a physician; but they did not have sense or sagacity enough for that, and as the laws now stand in any case where a married woman cannot safely become a mother, it is not possible for a physician *legally* to supply or direct means of prevention of conception, though *it is lawful,* should conception occur, for him *to produce abortion* to insure the mother's life, or rather to relieve her from the danger of a birth at full term. Behold, then, the result of laws based upon so-called moral sentiments instead of scientific reasoning; whereby prevention of conception is constituted an offence when abortion is not. Therefore if the laws were obeyed, the practical result would be a great number of abortions where contraception might serve instead; but the fact is that physicians and laymen take liberties with the law, and where it becomes a necessity to decide between lawful abortion and unlawful contraception, they prefer to break the man-made law against contraceptics rather than the natural law against abortion.

Foote went on to assert that Comstock's minions had protected from prosecution a drug store owned by a member of the Society for the Suppression of Vice, even though it sold the same contraceptive devices for which nearby druggists were arrested. Even more embarrassing was Foote's charge against Comstock's ally, Samuel Colgate, whose interests included promotion of vaseline. In sales literature used by Colgate was a letter from a San Rafael, California, physician informing doctors how to turn the ointment into a contraceptive. Foote left it an open question whether Colgate had violated a law he supported by sending this helpful bit of birth control information through the mails.

Foote's case, however, rested on more than wonderfully embarrassing revelations about vice-hunters, and he summarized briefly and usefully the chief points in a procontraceptive indictment of Comstockery:

We append the just reasons for our opposition to the present status of the laws of New York State, and several other states, as well as the Comstock postal law. We protest:

1st. That abortion is accorded a legitimate sphere while contraception is not—a provision manifestly impolitic, unnatural and immoral.

2nd. That the anti-contraceptic laws are not and cannot be effective in preventing vice (unchastity), because it is simply impossible to enforce them, and even if articles could not be sold in evasive ways, there are methods which no law can reach.

3rd. That if it were possible to enforce them and to suppress all knowledge as to methods, the result would be to discourage early marriage and to favor prostitution.

4th. That their effect thus far has been mainly to interrupt progress and reform in contraceptic arts, and to interfere with those who would make known to the masses the injurious effects of prevalent "conjugal sins."

5th. That they are daily disregarded or evaded by those whose only interest in so doing is for monetary gain, charging exorbitant prices for unreliable, unsatisfactory and hurtful drugs, chemicals or devices, all of which is made easy by the necessary excepting clause of the penal code concerning articles for prevention or treatment of disease.

6th. That all laws not in accord with popular favor, and therefore more honored in the breach than the observance, are a reproach to the government instituting them.

7th. That laws which are permitted for a long term of years to fall into the state of "innocuous desuetude," and then suddenly applied, as these have been, for moral effect, are too convenient engines of malice [particularly blackmail] and not "pro bono publico" [in the public interest].

8th. That laws restrictive of citizens' rights or invasive in purely family affairs, are not consistent with democratic government, and ought to be repealed.

9th. That these undemocratic restrictive laws are especially out of place in the United States, in view of the fact that no such laws have been enacted in Great Britain, Germany, France, Holland, Belgium or other continental kingdoms or republics of Europe.

Foote, in his moral justification of birth control, quoted his most ancient American predecessors, Robert Dale Owen and Dr. Charles Knowlton—an indication of how little had been changed in fifty-six years of controversy. There had, nonetheless, been some transformations since the appearance of Owen's Moral Physiology. *Foote drew upon better and more favorable medical knowledge than Owen or Knowlton possessed, although science in Foote's day still divided on the wisdom of sexual indulgence and on contraception's safety and effectiveness. Comstockery itself signified a new turn by banning birth control artifacts which could have been promoted earlier. This undoubtedly hindered contraceptive improvements (as Foote believed); but Comstock's forces also unwittingly publicized birth control by battling it in courts of law. Even more destructive to their own cause, they turned birth control into a civil liberties issue through persecution of advocates like the elder Dr.*

Foote. Thanks in large part to Anthony Comstock, contraception after 1873 was not simply a matter to be examined by the lights of moral and medical assumptions; it was a cause involving free speech as well as erotic expression.

Participants in nineteenth-century birth control controversies seldom asked the most important question: did their polemics make any difference? A declining birth rate, apparently not completely explicable otherwise, indicates that contraception probably was practiced on a significant scale. Yet the decline initially owed nothing to published sources because it appeared decades before the first American birth control tract. Comparison with Britain raises even more doubt that any simple relationship exists between birth control propaganda and rate of population growth. Despite the fact that England produced procontraceptive works well before the United States, English population increase turned downward later than ours, fully a half century after emergence of birth control books and pamphlets. The whole comparison, naturally, is complicated by any number of variables. America, for instance, began the nineteenth century with an extremely high birth rate, higher than Britain's, and some decline was inevitable. In addition, we really do not know precisely what happened to the social groups that came in contact with contraceptive and anticontraceptive literature, whether they had smaller or larger families than the general population. Still, it is difficult now to be confident that nineteenth-century birth control polemics changed many minds. More likely, the controversy worked its effects quite slowly, serving to comfort those already practicing contraception (probably for economic reasons), to accustom new generations to birth control sentiment, and to acquaint people with ever-evolving techniques.

Fully as significant as determining who won debates over contraception is the less obvious task of discovering the rules by which both sides played the game. Here the consensus was striking. By urging continence, late marriage, and infrequent intercourse, anticontraceptive writers promoted behavior that would have produced a lower birth rate just as surely as the semi-effective means birth control writers proposed—population limitation through restraint rather than contraception. For their part, birth control advocates, including radicals like John Humphrey Noyes, did not challenge the prevalent feeling that sex had to be guided carefully, by rationality rather than lust. Contraception, its defenders claimed, was merely a particularly sensible kind of guidance; it would not incite erotic license but rather would permit earlier marriage (hence less illicit sexual activity), and would save men and women from the poverty and suffering attendant on frequent childbearing.

Proponents of contraception generally agreed fully with their adversaries that chastity was worth maintaining, that "excess" was deplorable and destructive, that children were delightful, and that families were virtue's sanctuary. If birth control did open a breach in nineteenth-century morality's facade, it was unintentional and came about primarily through acceptance of nonreproductive erotic expression. The distance from Robert Dale Owen to "sexual freedom" is a century wide—Owen's assumptions about man's erotic nature were far closer to those of his enemies than to those of twentieth-century men and women carrying on the cause he pioneered.

---

1 The best guide to the history of contraception is still NORMAN E. HIMES' *Medical History of Contraception* (1936; rpt., New York: Shocken Books, 1970).

2 ROBERT DALE OWEN, *Moral Physiology; Or, A Brief and Plain Treatise on the Population Question* (London: J. Watson, 1841), pp. 17, 19–22.

3 CHARLES KNOWLTON, *Fruits of Philosophy. An Essay on the Population Question,* 2nd new ed. (London: Annie Besant and Charles Bradlaugh, n.d. [1877?]), p. 16.

4 E. B. FOOTE, JR., *The Radical Remedy in Social Science; Or, Borning Better Babies Through Regulating Reproduction by Controlling Conception* (New York: Murray Hill Publishing Co., 1886), pp. 20–21.

5 JOHN COWAN, *The Science of a New Life* (New York: Cowan & Company, Publishers, 1880), p. 133.

6 J. H. KELLOGG, *Plain Facts about Sexual Life* (Battle Creek, Michigan: Office of the Health Reformer, 1877), p. 159.

7 Cowan, *Science of a New Life,* pp. 108–109.

8 KELLOGG, *Plain Facts,* p. 167.

9 JOHN HUMPHREY NOYES, *Male Continence* (Oneida, New York: Office of Oneida Circular, 1872), pp. 5, 15, 18–20.

10 AUGUSTUS K. GARDNER, *The Conjugal Relationships as Regards Personal Health and Hereditary Well-Being Practically Treated,* 5th ed. (Glasgow: Thomas D. Morison, 1905), pp. 84–85, 88, 89, 99, 100, 106–109.

11 FOOTE, *Radical Remedy,* pp. 70–71, 72–73, 84, 88–89, 101–102.

CHAPTER NINE

Perfecting the Race

Rational control of sexuality, whether implying contraception, continence, or moderation, meant suppression of erotic impulses. But there was another aspect: a sense in nineteenth-century literature that sex, purged of its dangers and channeled properly, could be converted into a force for human betterment. Although advice-manual authors were guilty of exaggerating sensuality's perils, they also committed what was virtually the opposite sin—expecting too much of sex, expecting it to affect human betterment to a degree no physiological function can, no matter how firmly and morally controlled.

Biological laws joined theological commandments in nineteenth-century sexual morality, with injunctions such as "thou shalt not commit excess" taking their place alongside traditional mandates. In important ways, religion had prepared writers to accept certain kinds of scientific answers and to engage in certain lines of scientific investigation. Nowhere was this more apparent than in predictions about the ultimate result of proper sexual behavior. Religion's ancient answer—Divine pleasure—yielded, as the century went along, to that of Darwinian biology—improvement of mankind. Yet this new secular promise was credible to moralistic Americans partly because it emerged as logically from their theological assumptions as it did from biological science. Following a wave of revivalism in the 1820s, many evangelical Protestants had preached perfectionism, a doctrine varying from proponent to proponent but generally holding that man could approximate spiritual perfection while still on earth. It was not a long step to maintain that man might also achieve a corresponding physical perfection, becoming as free from bodily deformity as from sin.

One of the most reliable guides to the process was John Humphrey Noyes. Converted by revivalism, he became an incurable seeker. Following his theology and physiology with a literal-mindedness appalling to orthodox individuals, he eventually discovered salvation in the Oneida Community's "male continence" and "complex marriage." Noyes charted the smooth path from one sort of perfectionism to another—his own life eloquent testimony to the connection between evangelical enthusiasm and sexual experimentation. His remarks on the subject to William Hepworth Dixon, an English journalist, possessed both the perceptiveness of a shrewd observer and the authoritativeness of involvement.

It is evident from what we have seen that Revivals breed social revolutions.[1] All the social irregularities reported in the papers followed in the train of revivals; and, so far as I know, all revivals have developed tendencies to such irregularities. The philosophy of the matter seems to be this: Revivals are theocratic in their very nature; they introduce God into human affairs; the power that is supposed to be present in them is equivalent to inspiration and the power of miracles—that is to say, it is the actual Diety. In the conservative theory of Revivals, this power is restricted to the conversion of souls; but in actual experience it goes, or tends to go, into all the affairs of life. Revival preachers and Revival converts are necessarily in the incipient stage of a theocratic revolution; they have in their experience the beginning of a life under the Higher law; and if they stop at internal religious changes, it is because the influence that converted them is suppressed.

And the theocratic tendency, if it goes beyond religion, naturally runs first into some form of Socialism. Religious love is very near neighbor to sexual love, and they always get mixed in the intimacies and social excitements of Revivals. The next thing a man wants, after he has found the salvation of his soul, is to find his Eve and his Paradise. Hence these wild experiments and terrible disasters.

Noyes briefly discussed Shakerism and "bundling perfectionism," both demanding celibacy, and Mormonism, which initially was polygamous. All these, he concluded, "came out of the same fertile soil" of revivalism.

The course of things may be re-stated thus: Revivals lead to religious love; religious love excites the passions; the converts, finding themselves in theocratic liberty, begin to look about for their mates and their paradise. Here begins divergence. If women have to lead, the feminine idea that ordinary wedded love is carnal and unholy rises and becomes a ruling principle. Mating on the Spiritual plan, with all the heights and depths of sentimental love, becomes the order of the day. Then, if a prudent Mother Ann [leader of the Shakers] is at the head of affairs, the sexes are fenced off from each other, and carry on their Platonic intercourse through the grating. . . . On the other hand, if the leaders are men, the theocratic impulse takes the opposite direction, and polygamy in some form is the result. Thus Mormonism is the masculine form, as Shakerism is the feminine form, of the more morbid products of Revivals.

Our Oneida Socialism, too, is a masculine product of the great Revival.

Noyes exposed a very real tendency of the enthusiasm he had known in the 1830s. It frequently did gravitate from religious concern to earthly reforms, including monitoring relations between the sexes. But Noyes focused on extremes. Most evangelicals practiced neither absolute celibacy nor polygamy. Instead they combined sexual beliefs into broader programs to elevate mankind. Sylvester Graham, for instance, had been a clergyman before discovering the keys to glory in temperance, proper diet, and continence. Henry Clarke Wright, likewise a former minister, drifted through antislavery and Christian anarchism before authoring works on marriage and parentage which stressed sexual control and rationally guided reproduction. More respectable yet, Henry Ward Beecher, clerical son of a great revivalist, roared chaste pieties of all sorts for nearly half a century. Still, Noyes had a point. Revivalism and reform in antebellum America engendered faith that improvement of soul and body marched together and that progress depended on both.

Evangelical Protestantism was not the only current feeding the stream. Other prevalent kinds of thought presented reproduction and relations between men and women as means to social regeneration. Among these were some forms of mysticism popular in pre–Civil War America, including Swedenborgianism, an eighteenth-century cult which grew in popularity in the late 1840s. Followers of Emanuel Swedenborg, like their Swedish master, tended to communicate with spirits and angels and to place love and marriage in heaven's airy regions. Some, less scrupulous, found conjugal love's holiness to be an excuse to sample in search of a divinely appointed partner. But the purity of disciples like William Henry Holcombe was beyond doubt—Holcombe's conception of male/female relations was too abstract to be anything other than chaste. Yet Holcombe, and many of his fellow Swedenborgians, saw heavenly refinement of sexuality leading to human progress just as did exotic children of the Revival like John Humphrey Noyes.

A . . . grander use of marriage, and one running parallel with that of perfecting the individual character, is its use in the construction of a perfect society, a social millennium, the reign of Jesus Christ on earth. . . .[2]

It is a psychological law announced by Swedenborg, that *the state of conjugial love between man and woman, determines all other loves;* determines not only the joys of the married life, but the integrity, purity, wisdom of the parental love, the love of the neighbor and one's country, the love of the church and the Word; determines the nature of all the outflowing affections of the human spirit; determines, therefore, the entire civilization and outward condition of a people.

Give us individual regeneration; then let male and female regenerate souls be linked in holy wedlock, and we have the levers which will move and change the face of human society. The new era, the new life, the New Jerusalem, will begin in the closet, the chamber, the parlor, the home; and thence it will radiate like the sun in his glory, until it illumines and melts the world. . . .

The enlightenment of the mind and the purification of the heart in both sexes, and the proper organization, protection, and sanctification of marriage, are the great forces, operating from spiritual stand-points, which are to reorganize society. Whatever social, legal, political, or religious revolutions are necessary to give these forces their legitimate field and power, will inevitably be accomplished. Institutions, governments, churches, will all be modified or perish, if they impede the advance of the great truth that the married love and wisdom of Man and Woman are ultimately to govern the world.

Faith that marriage and reproduction, properly conducted, would improve mankind was not confined to evangelicals and mystics. Secular-minded Robert Dale Owen fully shared the day's spirit when, in 1830, he mused on contraception's potential for eliminating inherited disease, weakness, and deformity.

This view of the subject is to the physiologist, to the philosopher, to every friend of human improvement, a most interesting one.[3] "So long," to use the words of an eloquent lecturer, now in this city [Sylvester Graham], "as the tainted stream [of inheritance] is unhesitatingly transmitted through the channel of nature, from parent to offspring, so long will the text be verified which 'visits the sins of the fathers on the children, even to the third and fourth generation.'" And so long, I would add, will mankind (wise and successful whenever there is question of improving the animal races) be blind in perceiving, and listless in securing, that far nobler object, the physical, and thereby (in a measure) the mental and moral improvement of our own.

I may seem an enthusiast—and so let me seem then—when I express my conviction, that there is not a greater physical disparity between the dullest, shaggiest race of dwarf draught horses, and the fiery-spirited and silken-haired Arabian, than between man degenerate as he is, and man perfected as he might be: and though mental cultivation in this counts for much, yet organic melioration is an influential—an *indispensable* accessory.

In addition to the kind of secular reform represented by Owen, antebellum pseudo-science reinforced interest in improving man and society through rationally guided procreation and matrimony. Phrenology in particular exercised its genius for casting prevalent assumptions in empirical garb. One of phrenology's chief publicists, Lorenzo N. Fowler, benefited his readers (and perhaps their descendants) with advice on "hereditary influences." Fowler told prospective parents what sorts of "organizations" should and should not marry each other. After assessing the harm mothers and fathers could entail upon offspring, he broached the idea of encouraging procreation among the most desirable combinations, a subject that (he realized) would scandalize a portion of his readership.

Is it not absurd for anyone to advance the opinion, that it is too *delicate* a subject to improve the human race; while at the same time the animal kingdom is thought to be of such vital importance? [4] Great pains are taken to improve our breeds of horses and sheep—papers are published, books circulated, and much said and done on this subject—those individuals who are quite active in these stock improvements being looked upon as very public-spirited men. Even the hog is not exempt from these attempts at improvement, and very successful have they been too. But man, the noblest work of God, made in His own image and likeness, possessed of an immortal mind, heir to a future existence, and having charge over these animals, must be allowed to go on, gather strength in impurity and imperfections, and grow more imperfect daily, because of a proper *delicacy*. How excessively inconsistent—as though, if it were improper for us to become acquainted with these laws, it would still be necessary for us to understand them so as properly to discharge the duties which devolve on us as parents.

If it be *really too delicate* to discuss the principles necessary to be known and observed before one is qualified to enter on the duties incident to this change of condition—then, it is most certainly entirely *too delicate* to be married, and absolutely *shocking* to become parents. . . .

The true *nature of the case* is: The means for continuing the existence of man are put into *our* hands, and if we use them *properly,* we shall have the blessings of Providence as a matter of course; but, if we abuse this power, the *curse* will rest on our own heads, and our children will suffer the consequences. Society, generally, has been wrapped in cloaks of ignorance and innocence long enough.

We most certainly have obeyed the command to increase and multiply; but, in a most reckless, unprincipled, and impious manner, without having paid any regard whatever to many of the principles established by Almighty Power, as guides for our conduct in these transactions.

That you may see the truth of what has been stated, and feel its force, you have only to look into the bosoms of your own families, or of your acquaintance, and notice the difference between those who obey the laws of their organization and those who do not. Observe what kind of children they severally send into the world. Mark the degree of health, perfection, and happiness there is in those families, when compared and you will not fail to forget the delicacy of the subject in contemplation of its vast importance.

Religious perfectionism, secular reform, pseudo-science, and folk wisdom assured antebellum Americans that children inherited their parents' strengths and defects. An incorrigible zeal to improve things encouraged Lorenzo Fowler and others to draw, at least in print, the obvious conclusion: human beings could breed for progress. It was left for John Humphrey Noyes' Oneida Community actually to put theory into practice. In 1869 the colony embarked upon an experiment in "stirpculture": particularly impressive men and women mated to produce even more gifted offspring. (Noyes himself fathered nine of those born in the next decade.) By 1869, however, the pre–Civil War period's loosely formulated hereditarian thought was giving way to more empirical and more coherent theory. Charles Darwin's Origin of Species, *published in 1859, powerfully defended the idea that species evolve in time, a matter Darwin explained in terms of spontaneously arising variations and as a process of natural selection by which characteristics conducive to survival pass on to progeny. Other British writers, notably*

Herbert Spencer and Francis Galton, applied their understanding of Darwinian biology to human development, where it also seemed nature's laws held sway and where it appeared as if only the most fit should survive and reproduce. Appropriately, Noyes read this literature, assimilating it with the Protestant perfectionism that decades earlier set him off on his strange pilgrimage. In Noyes' justification of Oneida's "Scientific Propagation," antebellum enthusiasm and post–Civil War biological and social science converged.

The vital center of sociology, toward which all eyes are turning, is the science which presides over reproduction.[5] It is becoming clear that the foundations of scientific society are to be laid in the scientific propagation of human beings. . . .

[Darwin's] object was to establish a theory looking backward to the origin of species, but the practical result of his labors has been to establish a theory looking forward to the duty of scientific propagation. His great theme is the plasticity of living forms. He shows, first, how nature alone, in the countless ages of the past, has slowly transmuted plants and animals; then how the unsystematic care of man, since the dawn of intelligence, has hastened these changes; and finally how modern science and skill have rapidly perfected the races that are subservient to human use. . . .

Phrenologists, popular physiologists and reformers of various kinds have long been busy carrying over the laws of Darwin into the public conscience, translating analogy into application; and it is remarkable how common it has become for books and newspapers to acknowledge the duty of scientific propagation, and confess that in this matter "we are all miserable sinners. . . ."

There can be no rational doubt that the laws of physiology are in general the same for man as for other animals. Indeed the most important of these laws, so far as our present subject is concerned, has just been scientifically fastened upon man by Mr. [Francis] Galton. He demonstrates that not only the physical qualities of individuals and races, but their intellectual, artistic, and moral characteristics, and even their spiritual proclivities, are as transmissible as the speed of horses. There can be no doubt that if it were possible for men and women to be directed in their propagation by superior beings, as animals are, or by their own sincere enthusiasm for science, the results of suppressing the poorest and breeding from the best would be the same for them as for cattle and sheep. There can be no doubt that, if it were compatible with public morality and with the proper care of women and children, to "give special privileges to the most exalted individuals in the perpetuation of the species," as the English journal of science suggested, the elevation of the human species would be as rapid as that of any of the lower races. Indeed the difference between the sexes in regard to the power of reproduction, which is the reason for special selection of males, is even wider in the case of man than in that of horses; and, though existing institutions wholly ignore it, we may be sure that, in the nature of things, it gives man superior possibilities of improvement of blood. Finally, there can be no doubt that by segregating superior families, and by breeding them in and in, superior varieties of human beings might be produced which would be comparable to the thoroughbreds in all the domestic races.

Noyes' program brought him into direct conflict with the most cherished pieties of his day. The "institution of marriage," *he cheerfully conceded,* "is an absolute bar to scientific propagation." *He further condemned* "the tendency of high-toned moralists . . . to extend the domain of the law of incest, and so make all approach to scientfic propagation as difficult as possible." *Having assaulted matrimony and urged incest, he did make his bow to sentimental conventions.*

Institutions of the future . . . must not injure HOME. Here we touch another point of difference between the cases of animals and human beings. Man has a social nature that demands very different treatment from that of animals. The best part of human happiness consists in sexual and parental love, and the best part of human education consists in the training of these passions in the school of home. That school must not be superseded or weakened by the new arrangements, but must be honored more than ever.

Can this be done consistently with the changes which scientific propagation requires? That is the hard question which science has now to solve. We offer but a hint toward its solution. If home could be enlarged to the scale, for instance, of the Shaker families, and if men and women could be taught to enjoy love that stops short of propagation, and if all could learn to love other children than their own, there would be nothing to hinder scientific propagation in the midst of homes far better than any that now exist. . . .

Though it must be conceded that, in the present state of human passions and institutions, there are many and great difficulties in the way of our going back to the natural simplicity of the Hebrew fathers [whom Noyes thought inbred] or forward to the scientific simplicity of the cattle-breeders, yet it is important to know and remember that these difficulties are not physiological, but sentimental. As the old theologians used to say, our inability to obey the law of God is not natural, but moral. We are too selfish and sensual and ignorant to do for ourselves what we have done for animals, and we have surrounded ourselves with institutions corresponding to and required by our selfishness and sensuality and ignorance. But for all that we need not give up the hope of better things, at least in some far-off future. If the difficulties in our way were natural and physiological, no amount of science or grace could ever overcome them; but as they are only passional and institutional, we may set the very highest standard of thorough-breeding before us as our goal, and believe that every advance of civilization and science is carrying us toward it.

Noyes' talent was for extremism—his version of "scientific propagation" could scarcely have been more repugnant to proper morality. Yet his assumptions were not so very different from those eventually adopted by respectable men and women enlisting under the banner of eugenics, a term coined by Francis Galton. Supporters of eugenics maintained that the best stock should reproduce and thus perfect the race, while inferior human beings should be discouraged (or prevented) from having offspring. Such doctrines only became prominent toward the end of the nineteenth century, when a number of writers fretted over the possibility of "race suicide" as the birth rate of immigrants and other purportedly less favored types shot rapidly above that of "superior" people (namely, educated and propertied white Protestants). At its height, the eugenics movement attracted notable Americans, among them Alexander Graham Bell, inventor of the telephone, and David Starr Jordan, president of Stanford University. By 1910 there was a privately run Eugenics Record Office at Cold Harbor, Long Island, backed by Mrs. E. H. Harriman's considerable wealth; and the language of fit and unfit, inferior and superior races had filtered into political rhetoric, including Theodore Roosevelt's. By 1917 sixteen states had laws permitting sterilization of certain kinds of unfortunates presumed capable of passing on hereditary defects. But eugenics' days of glory came long after Noyes' death, and much of the movement's popularity was among staid middle- and upper-class men and women who detested moral radicals like Noyes.

❧

Despite the claims of "scientific" truth Noyes, eugenicists, and others made, nineteenth-century hereditarian thought flourished in something of a free enterprise atmosphere; writers bought and sold theory as the market would bear, with little systematically gathered evidence to hinder them. Until comparatively recent developments in genetic science there has not been reliable knowledge as to what characteristics truly can be passed along to children, nor has there been much good information about the mechanisms by which traits are acquired and transmitted.

Consequently, advice-manual authors well into the twentieth century were free to present their own preferred lists of inheritable diseases and defects, including personal and moral attributes that actually are products of environment and culture. Some authorities went so far as to insist that virtually every act by either parent during gestation, as well as prior to conception, could affect progeny drastically. Lacking the restraint genetic knowledge might have imposed, Dr. John Harvey Kellogg depicted an impressive array of ways even parents of basically sound stock could affect their unborn children.

Human beings are generated in as haphazard and reckless a manner as weeds are sown by the wind.[6] No account is taken of the possible influence which may be exerted upon the future destiny of the new being by the physical or mental condition of parents at the moment when the germ of life is planted, by the mental and physical conditions and surroundings of the mother while the young life is developing. . . .

Who can tell how many of the liars, thieves, drunkards, murderers, and prostitutes of our day are less responsible for their crimes against themselves, against society, and against Heaven, than those who were instrumental in bringing them into the world? Almost every village has its boy "who was born drunk," a staggering, simpering, idiotic representative of a drunken father, beastly intoxicated at the very moment when he should have been most sober.

It is an established physiological fact that the character of offspring is influenced by the mental as well as the physical conditions of the parents at the moment of the performance of the generative act. In view of this fact, how many parents can regard the precocious—or even mature—manifestations of sexual depravity in their children without painful smitings of conscience at seeing the legitimate results of their own voluptuousness? By debasing the reproductive function to an act of selfish animal indulgence, they imprinted upon their children an almost irresistible tendency to vice. Viewing the matter from this stand-point, what wonder that licentiousness is rife! that true chastity is among the rarest virtues! . . .

It cannot be doubted that the throngs of deaf, blind, crippled, idiotic unfortunates who were "born so," together with a still larger class of dwarfed, diseased, and constitutionally weak individuals, are the lamentable results of the violation of some sexual law on the part of their progenitors. . . .

In concluding the subject, we may summarize its chief points as follows, for the purpose of impressing them more fully upon the mind:

1. If a child is begotten in lust, its lower passions will as certainly

be abnormally developed as peas will produce peas, or potatoes produce potatoes. If the child does not become a rake or a prostitute, it will be because of uncommonly fortunate surroundings, or a miracle of divine grace. . . .

2. The same remarks apply with equal force to the transmission of other qualities. If the interest of the parents is only for self, with no thought for the well-being of the one whose destiny is in their hands, they can expect naught but a selfish character, a sordid, greedy disposition, in the child.

3. The influence of the father is, at the outset, as great as that of the mother. The unhappy or immoral thoughts of one alone at the critical moment when life is imparted, may fix for eternity a foul blot upon a character yet unformed.

4. If during gestation the mother is fretful, complaining, and exacting; if she requires to be petted and waited upon; if she gratifies every idle whim and indulges every depraved desire and perverted appetite—as thousands of mothers do—the result will surely be a peevish, fretful child that will develop into a morose and irritable man or woman, imperious, unthankful, disobedient, willful, gluttonous, and vicious.

Kellogg, who was later deeply involved in the eugenics movement, expressed in biological language an ancient fear that the sins of fathers will haunt posterity. Reproduction in a Darwinian world, no less than in a biblical one, had cosmic significance, affecting remote generations, involving parents and children in guilt for each other's failings. Although exaggerated, Kellogg's position deserves more respect than its physiological obsolesence seems to merit. He did, it is true, radically underestimate the power of environment and culture to shape personality; and—unfortunately—hereditarian thought such as his served racism and elitism. Still, we have not passed so far beyond him that we are absolutely certain what characteristics can be inherited, despite decades of extensive investigation. In addition, present-day authorities have come back to an appreciation of effects upon the unborn of such factors as a mother's diet during gestation, or, tragically, her drug addiction. Kellogg was badly wrong on details, but he was not wrong to worry about prenatal influences. And he gave good counsel when he insisted that men and women look to themselves, to their physical condition and situation in life before bearing children. Furthermore, the fearfulness and guilt implicit in Kellogg's beliefs were balanced by an invincible optimism: depraved as humans were, they could be perfected; sinful as they were, they could learn to direct their passions to the cause of social betterment. Advisers like Dr. Kellogg, who seem glumly anti-sexual, actually shared, in a curious way, the faith of nineteenth-century reformers that man's lowest impulses could be transcended in human-kind's quest for progress.

Darwinian biology gave strength and direction to hereditarian thought, but—as far as advice manuals were concerned—it produced differences of degree, not kind. As early as 1830, twenty-nine years before Origin of Species, *Robert Dale Owen argued that reproduction could be used for improvement of mankind and of society. On this particular point the message (although not the vocabulary) of advice literature remained remarkably constant: perfection of human beings could come about through refinement and control of erotic impulses. Yet the scope of concern did narrow somewhat following the Civil War, with social crusades becoming less prominent. Many antebellum panaceas remained vital—temperance and diet, in particular—but evolution encouraged moral guides (at least temporarily) to find their field of endeavor in personal relationships and to put their ultimate faith for progress on natural laws promising inexorably to weed out sin and weakness, rather than on collective action. Antebellum figures like Robert Dale Owen, or even John Humphrey Noyes, sought energetically to transform economic, institutional, and social conditions, as well as to put sensuality in its place. In contrast, Dr. John Cowan's post–Civil War perfectionism limited itself, more passively and more restrictedly, to faith that families could accomplish reformation.*

The impartial observer and thinker will allow that two-thirds, if not three-fourths, of the misery of the world arises from the infelicity of the conjugal relations; and to no single country or nation is it confined, but it pervades all society the world over. . . .[7]

That marriage, consummated under right conditions, for right purposes, bears intimately on the prosperity and welfare of communities and states, and is the source of all industry, subordination and government among men, the author firmly believes. . . .

Closely allied to a true and perfect marriage is the command to increase and multiply—a command that, among the better and higher classes of society, is in danger of being sadly neglected. Its importance in the solution of life's problems—the hopes and fears, pleasures and pains, health and sickness, prosperity and adversity—is not lightly to be estimated. In the propagating of the species knowingly and understandingly, the father and mother can do more toward a true solution of the questions of the age, than can all the temperance societies, religious denominations, and reform institutions in the world. Parents, exercising a lovable and true use of this life-giving power—the power of creating man in God's own image—can, if they earnestly will and work for it, recreate and people the world with mortals just, pure, loving and Christ-like. A great and arduous responsibility rests on every father and mother who entertain the desire of bringing into life a new being, but it is a responsibility which, if exercised as unperverted nature intended it to be, brings with it naught but ineffable pleasure, holy joy, and unalloyed happiness.

Cowan's "Science of a New Life," promulgated in 1869, received the "very cordial approval" *of William Lloyd Garrison, who had spent his most active decades working in "reform institutions" like those Cowan's remedy presumed to supplant. But Garrison's praise marked more of a change in emphasis than a renunciation of earlier reform activities. There had always been an anarchistic streak in Garrison and among people who sought change in the pre–Civil War period, a desire to reach the human body and heart directly, without state or church as intermediaries. Belief in reproduction's redemptive power was fully consistent with this drive because it assumed that men and women, not governments and sects, were competent to bring about the millennium. Yet, to pin faith on the family and on procreation was to place responsibility for progress on individuals rather than on institutions, social structure, and environment—in other words, it was to miss many real issues.*

Dr. Elizabeth Blackwell, like Garrison, had grown up with antebellum reform, winning an early battle for woman's rights in 1849, when she became the first professionally educated American female physician. From the mellower perspective of 1879, Dr. Blackwell found the cause of civilization to reside in sex and in the home, not in challenging the social order. The job of perfecting mankind, despite having acquired a new terminology, seemed (much as it had a half century earlier) to begin with moral control over the body's sinful urges. By 1879, however, race betterment and national glory had nearly supplanted social justice and God's favor as rewards for success.

The records of history confirm the teaching of physiology and observation, in relation to the fundamental character of sexual virtue, as the secret of durable national greatness.[8] The decline of all the great nations of antiquity is marked by the prevalence of gross social corruption. The complex effects of the same cause are strikingly observed in the condition of the Mohammedan and other Eastern races, and in all the tribes subject to them. We find amongst these races, as the result of their sexual customs, a want of human charity. . . .

The value of a nation, its position in the scale of humanity, its durability, must always be judged by the condition of its masses; and the test of that condition is the strength and purity of home virtues—the character of the women of the nation. . . .

The great lesson derived from history . . . is always this—viz., that moral development must keep pace with the intellectual, or the race degenerates. This moral element is especially embodied by women, and purity in woman cannot exist without purity in man; this weighty truth being shown by the facts already stated, viz., by the action of licentiousness upon the great mass of unprotected women, by its re-action upon other classes, and by the accumulating influence of hereditary sensuality. . . .

We learn that the early and faithful union of one man with one woman is the true ideal of society. It secures the health and purity of the family relation, and is the foundation of social and national welfare. It is supported by sound principles of physiology, by historical study of the rise and fall of nations, and by a consideration of the evils of our present age.

The lessons of the past and present, our clearer knowledge of cause and effect, alike prove the wisdom of the highest religious teaching, viz., that the faithful union of strong and pure young manhood and womanhood is the only element out of which a strong and durable nation can grow.

Religious duty, patriotism, and biological imperatives converged in Dr. Blackwell's scheme of things: parenthood by physiologically and morally fit men and women became a form of worship and a prop for national pride. Farther removed from millennialism and Darwinism, and bearing memories of Nazi genetic chauvinism, few recent writers would dare make such claims for procreation, preferring to consider sex as a part of individual fulfillment, not a means to racial betterment, human perfection, or American greatness.

❧

Although nineteenth-century advice-manual authors commonly began circumspectly, approaching the delicate subject of sex with trepidation, they often ended with brazen faith in the power of sexual activity (rightly guided) to improve mankind. Tension between the wary beginning and the optimistic conclusion was only one of many signs of stress appearing in sexual advice given by American writers. Authors frequently idealized woman, partly because of her supposedly unlascivious nature, and yet feared female seductiveness; they fretted about the dreadful effects of sexual expressiveness and yet glorified marriage, the institution giving legitimacy to sexual expressiveness; they delighted in children and yet advocated behavior that would produce fewer children. And, of course, there was the final irony—belief that sexuality, even though a dangerous impulse, could be rationally controlled and turned toward creation of a better future for the race. It is, nevertheless, not surprising that nineteenth-century advice literature had its tensions and ironies; these may well be inherent in moral pronouncements of any sort. Codes of conduct, after all, function in part to mediate conflicts within individual consciences and conflicts between individuals and society, a thankless process of reconciling opposing forces.

Assessment of advice literature should not stop with discovery of its inevitable tensions. Instead one must go a step farther and seek to comprehend what compels particular groups, at particular historical moments, to have their own special sets of concerns—their own peculiar tensions. The job here, then, is to understand why nineteenth-century American works on sexual matters developed certain themes and arrived at a limited number of conclusions, themes and conclusions rather different from those of earlier generations and decidedly different from those of twentieth-century authorities. At present we really do not know with great assurance why nineteenth-century moralists expressed the sexual attitudes they did; and the ultimate answer will not be found in their writings alone—although such books are indispensable first sources. Yet outlines of an answer do emerge when we compare the general messages of nineteenth-century advisers with the world of middle-class men and women who made up the bulk of their reading public. It was a rapidly transforming world, expanding territorially, economically, and even politically, as immigration and less restrictive voting requirements brought new kinds of people into the political process. It was a world in which traditional sources of moral authority, particularly churches and government, were badly divided and (in the case of government) suddenly opened to vulgar men whom more severe consciences regarded as immoral. To make things worse, there were dreadful temptations to sin, especially for new dwellers in America's booming cities, now cut off from the moral scrutiny endemic to small towns.

It would be easy to imagine that repressive sexual pronouncements were simply the response of anxiety-ridden moralists, disturbed by rapid change and fearfully aware that the old ethical order was challenged. There is truth to such an interpretation; advice manual authors were painfully sensitive to threats social fluidity posed to morality. There was, however, more to nineteenth-century life than fear and a determination to impose order upon a rowdy society and upon rowdy instincts. The most enduring Victorian artifacts—buildings, art, and fiction—testify to still other attitudes: fancifulness (frequently the cumbersome fancy of Victorian gothic, but fancy nonetheless), a reverence for prosperity, and a smug conviction that the nineteenth century represented the summit of human comfort, wisdom, and progress. People who made and admired these buildings, works of art, and pieces of fiction were not dominated by fear in any obvious way. It seems most likely that for them a balance had been struck between anxieties generated by change and a middle-class admiration for the material benefits of change. Sexual advice literature sought a complementary kind of stability, allowing people who followed its prescriptions to believe that, no matter what disorders existed in society, they could control the most intimate aspects of their existence—their bodies and their lusts. In addition, sexual restraint promised to reconcile erotic drives with economic advancement by reassuring men and women that they ought not to produce large (and costly) families, and by encouraging concentration of energy into work rather than sensual indulgence. People who achieved the discipline demanded by advice-manual authors were capable of resisting the licentious diversions their vigorous society offered; and their stern self-mastery made them equally capable of the precision and dedication an emerging industrial order required and rewarded.

Judged by present-day orthodoxy, nineteenth-century advice literature appears naïve. It drew upon faulty biological knowledge and its grand promises of human perfection seem to have been illusions, maybe even dangerous illusions because they depended upon harsh suppression of sexual impulses and implied planned reproduction of a sort that took on ugly class and racial overtones. Beyond that—to complete a bill of indictment—nineteenth-century sexual morality undoubtedly caused suffering and guilt among those who failed to meet its demands. There are, nevertheless, things to say in defense of nineteenth-century advice-manual authors. They conveyed messages appropriate to their times and they helped men and women conquer their most anarchical urges, leading them to believe they had gained control over a small corner of their rapidly evolving environment. That was, for some people, a genuine gain—whether it came at too high a cost is another matter. And yet the twentieth century's record gives little reason for self-congratulation. There is no evidence that our scientific discoveries and our emancipation from some nineteenth-century beliefs have created happier, more productive human beings. Persistence of sexual prejudices, frustrations, and anxieties are reminders that our enlightenment may not be markedly superior to that of our ancestors—that we have not been a great deal more successful than previous generations in solving problems of human fulfillment.

---

[1] WILLIAM HEPWORTH DIXON, *Spiritual Wives* (Philadelphia: J. B. Lippincott & Co., 1868), pp. 347–48, 351. There is something of a textual prob-

lem with this letter, which was dated March 1867. Dixon admitted that "In a few places I have altered a word and even struck out a phrase. . . ." Other evidence from Noyes makes it probable that Dixon was correct when claiming he had "in no case changed the sense, or even veiled the meaning meant to be conveyed by the reverend gentleman."

2 William H. Holcombe, *The Sexes Here and Hereafter* (Philadelphia: J. B. Lippincott & Co., 1869), pp. 257–60.

3 Robert Dale Owen, *Moral Physiology; A Brief and Plain Treatise on the Population Question* (London: J. Watson, 1841), pp. 21–22.

4 L. N. Fowler, *Marriage: Its History and Ceremonies; with a Phrenological and Physiological Exposition of the Functions and Qualifications for Happy Marriages,* 22nd ed. (New York: Fowlers and Wells Publishers, 1853), pp. 193–95.

5 J. H. Noyes, *Essay on Scientific Propagation* (Oneida, N.Y.: Office of Oneida Circular, n.d.), pp. 3, 4–5, 21, 25, 26, 31, 24.

6 J. H. Kellogg, *Plain Facts About Sexual Life* (Battle Creek, Michigan: Office of the Health Reformer, 1877), pp. 64–69.

7 Dr. John Cowan, *The Science of a New Life* (New York: Cowan & Company, Publishers, 1880), pp. 20–21.

8 Dr. Elizabeth Blackwell, *Counsel to Parents on the Moral Education of Their Children* (New York: Brentano's Literary Emporium, 1879), pp. 76–77, 79, 81–82.

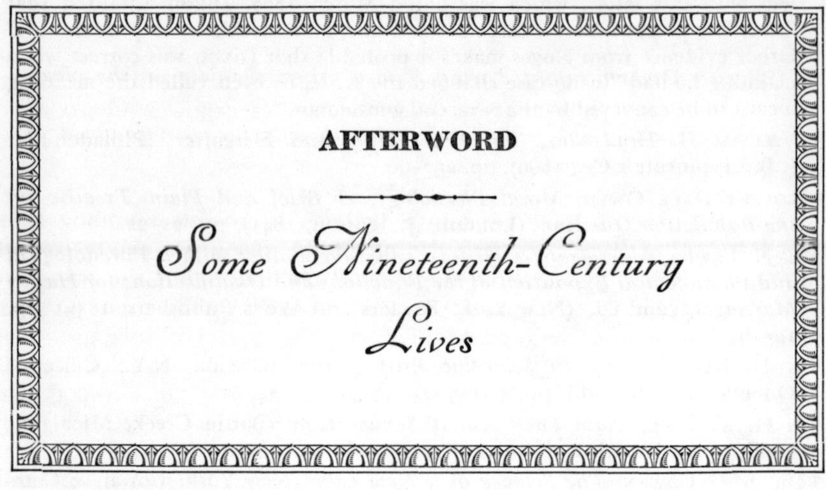

AFTERWORD

Some Nineteenth-Century Lives

Nineteenth-century authors were wont to illustrate dire warnings and miraculous cures with case histories and testimonials from clients. Despite the obvious danger of taking these vignettes too literally, they, better than any other aspect of advice literature, show the effects of moral preachments upon living men and women.

Lorenzo Fowler used a young man's sad experience to convince his readers that rational mate choice, particularly through phrenology, could prevent unhappiness (and disillusionment).

A gentleman in Lowell, Mass., married a lady who had a large and splendid head, and supposed she had a body equally large and healthy to support it.[1] He was informed by a Phrenologist that the head was too large for the size of the body, but *he* thought otherwise; for, to all appearances, her bust was fully developed; but, to his surprise, after they were married, he found that her fine form and plumpness was *more than half cloth;* forgetting, I suppose, that Lowell was a manufacturing town, and that there was an abundance of raw material that could be moulded into the outward semblance of vitality by the milliner's hand.

THE BAD . . .

Sylvester Graham reported word from a prison chaplain on the physical condition of inmates under his care. The clergyman gave this novel interpretation of the pallor and ill health afflicting men confined to nineteenth-century jails:

Self-pollution, I have reason to believe, is universal among prisoners.[2] One of them, who has the means of forming a pretty correct judgment in the matter, told me he had no doubt that the prisoners were as regular in that practice as they were in taking their suppers. Some of them greatly injured their health by the indulgence. Not long since, as I was passing the cell of one of the prisoners, just at twilight, he spoke to me with a low and tremulous voice and downcast look. "I shan't live long," said he; "don't you see how poor I am growing? my flesh has almost gone off my bones." I observed that what he said was true. When I first knew him, he had a full and ruddy cheek; now it was pale and sunken. I suspected the cause, and made inquiries accordingly. He confessed that he had become a slave to that vice, and feared it was doing him harm; but did not dare to speak to the doctor about it, and did not know that he could avoid it—"for," said he, "I seem to have no power over myself. I awake from my sleep, and find myself in the act. Three times a night, for weeks in succession, I have yielded to it, and frequently without being voluntary in the thing." He evinced clearly the reciprocal influence between the brain and genital organs.

There are several others in prison whom I know to be given up to a similar excess; and without exception, they all have that cadaverous look, bloodless lips, impaired memory, bodily weakness and pain, and those internal complaints, of which Mr. G. [Sylvester Graham] speaks in his Lecture.

. . . AND THE SUCCESSFUL

So insidious was sex that it could strike down an individual at any moment, even in the prime of life and good fortune.

C. N. commenced the practice of self-pollution very young; and before he was aware of its ruinous effects, he had nearly destroyed his constitution.[3] As soon as his eyes were opened, however, to his error, and the danger of his situation, he abandoned the mischievous practice with horror and remorse. By long perseverance in strictly virtuous habits, he regained a very good degree of health and enjoyment; but he was never able so completely to overcome the effects of his former error, as to give to his system that constitutional vigour, and power of endurance and resistance, which belong to those who have never greatly violated the laws of their nature. Soon after he came of age, he was established in a prosperous and lucrative business; and at a suitable time, he became the husband of a very amiable and excellent wife, who, in about two years after their marriage, presented him with a lovely son. He was truly an amiable, intelligent, prosperous, and happy man—dearly beloved in his family, and highly esteemed by all who knew him. In the flood-tide of his prosperity, he forgot the duties which he owed to his own body. A prodigious pressure of successful business so engrossed and excited his mind, that his regular meals were not properly attended to; and he encroached so much upon his hours of rest, that he was very frequently up, and his mind intensely employed, till eleven, twelve, and one o'clock at night; and then he retired to bed with his mind in such a state of excitement, that he found it impossible to sleep for one or two hours after he retired. In this manner he held on, and held out, till the extreme pressure of his business was over, and the season terminated in the highest prosperity. Everything had gone exactly as he wished, and he had been the gainer of several thousand dollars. But amidst all this prosperity, he had excessively over-worked his nervous system, and now, when he was no longer excited by his extraordinary stimulus of his business, he suddenly sunk down into a state of extreme nervous exhaustion, and consequent mental depression. A high degree of morbid irritability and sympathy supervended, and a dark and cheerless gloom came over his mind. Medical assistance was called, and the attempt was made to raise him by the free use of high-seasoned flesh-meat, porter, wine, &c., all of which served only to aggravate his sufferings and plunge him deeper into darkness and despair. In this state of things I saw him. His misery exceeded all description. It was impossible to divert his mind from his affliction for a single moment. He continually exclaimed, in the most heart-rending tones—"I am lost! I am lost! I have destroyed myself! I have committed the unpardonable sin; and nothing but perdition awaits me." When I tried to break the spell of his mind, and to arouse him to other thoughts, he replied, in the deepest dejection and despair—"It is of no use—it is too late! I am a ruined man! my soul is sealed to eternal perdition! I have destroyed myself; and why should I live any longer, to heap up my already overflowing measure of wrath, and anguish, and horror? I cannot—I will not live." With much difficulty, I succeeded in drawing out from him a disclosure of what he considered the cause of all his misery. He said that in his youth he had indulged in the awful sin of self-pollution, till it had ruined his constitution; and that he was perfectly certain that, in so doing, he had committed an unpardonable sin. I strove in vain to convince him that his mind was extremely affected by the condition of his nervous system. "It is of no use," he replied, "I know that my damnation is sure! God will never forgive such abominable sins. There is no redemption—no hope for me; and I will live no longer in this state of despair and anguish." We are obliged to watch him every moment, to keep him from destroying his own life. And by abstracting from this diet his wine, porter, flesh, and every other heating and stimulating substance, and putting him strictly upon a very plain, unstimulating farinaceous diet, together with the tepid bath in the evening, just before going to bed, and the cold shower bath in the morning, and free exercise in the open air, he was gradually restored to health of body and mind, and to the full enjoyment of himself, his family, and his friends; and remained, as he had been before, a useful and much esteemed member of society, and a worthy member of a religious community.

UNDUE CONTINENCE

It is possible to overdo a good thing and some authorities, Dr. Frederick Hollick among them, were sure that it was no better to remain absolutely celibate than it was to commit excess.

The subject of this case was a Lawyer, aged thirty-one, of good constitution, and of active Temperament.[4] When he applied to me his general health was not much affected, but from various unusual symptoms he had begun to be somewhat alarmed.

I found on enquiry that he was naturally very amative, but at the same time *very prudent,* and uncommonly fond of money. He had made up his mind not to marry till he had secured a *fortune,* and was able to support a family in good *style*. This he expected to do before he was forty, and in the mean time sexual gratification was to be foresworn.

His fear of consequences, and of exposure, kept him from illicit intercourse, except very rarely, and he had too much good sense to practice self abuse, except when quite young. He entertained the notion, as many others do, that his reproductive powers could be held in abeyance as it were, and yet be found ready when he could *afford* to employ them. In fact I have no doubt but he promised himself extra indulgence then to make up for his prudential restraint.

The only serious inconvenience experienced up to his twenty-eighth year was nightly emissions, which somewhat affected his mind, making him, as he expressed it, not quite so bright as usual. These however became gradually less frequent, but the effects *increased!* His memory especially began to fail, and also his *power of application,* so that he had to *drive* himself to his work, instead of making it a pleasure, as formerly.

At times he would feel nearly as well and energetic as ever he did, but then would follow a period of terrible depression and languor, which he was strongly tempted to relieve by using stimulants, but fortunately did not.

His consolation was in thinking that he could keep on at least as well as he was, until the hoped for period of his retirement, when all would come right again. The symptoms had however become so much more strongly marked, and his periods of depression, or fits of the *horrors* as he called them, so much more frequent, and so much longer in their duration, that he began to fear he might be *too far gone* to recover. . . .

His sexual powers had become considerably impaired, but still were capable of renovation, by judicious treatment and conduct, if such renovation were advisable. It would however have been useless to restore his powers unless they were to be naturally employed, because they would otherwise fail again worse than ever.

In spite of all however, he determined to try his powers of endurance still further, and accordingly procured a *Nervous stimulant* which was recommended to him and kept on as before. I lost sight of him for about nine months, and then receiving a letter dated from a celebrated water-cure establishment, informing me that he was *worse,* and that he would shortly come on to consult me again.

The Letter states—"I found myself so much worse about four months ago that I was compelled to leave my business, and abandon the medication I had till then persisted in. In my despair I came on here, to try the *cure all* treatment, but to my sorrow it has failed also. I am worse and *growing worse!* You can have no idea my dear sir what I have suffered, and yet with little or no bodily ailing, at least none that is very apparent. Day after day have I sat in my office trying in vain to *fix my mind* on a case. I could not do it to save my life. My mind would fly to the stars or to the depths of the sea, or even lose itself altogether, but *would not* fix upon what I wished to study. . . .

My head has also begun to pain me, especially in the back part of it, and is constantly *full* and heavy, as if packed with *lead*—my eyes often become dim, and a rushing sound fills my ears, till I become quite confused. Latterly also I have suffered considerably from palpitation of the heart, and my bowels and stomach are quite irregular in their action. The emissions I have not seen now for six months, and this I think must be a good sign. I am however troubled with a very frequent desire to urinate, and my water is often thick and cloudy.

Now my dear Doctor I am determined to follow your advice, *providing* you can sufficiently restore me! There however is a new apprehension, my sexual powers and desires have decidedly lessened, especially since I have used the cold water, and I begin to fear I never *can* marry—in which case I say solemnly *I do not want to live!*"

On seeing this Gentleman I found he really had, as he remarked, gone *down hill* at a rapid rate, and I by no means felt sanguine of his recovery. From his excellent constitution however, and from his not having been exhausted by excesses of any kind, I did not despair, but put him at once under proper treatment.

The *worst* sign was precisely that which he thought the *best,* namely the stopping of the *nightly emissions.* I suspected at once that the discharges still occurred, but in another and unseen form, much more dangerous. I explained to him how, in such cases, the semen began at last to flow out *with the urine,* by which means so much was lost that the ordinary emissions ceased altogether. This was a new light to him, and he at once called to mind a number of symptoms which seemed to prove my position. To make it certain however I at once submitted a portion of the urine to microscopical examination, as is my custom, and the result left no doubt as to the existence of the trouble. The urine in the morning contained an immense quantity of semen, and I found that more or less escaped every time the bladder was emptied. . . .

The first thing to be done was to remove the irritability and relaxation of the seminal Ducts, which was the immediate cause of the semen flowing out with the urine. This was effected by *Cauterizing,* the case being one which properly admitted of that operation. The result was perfectly satisfactory, the urinary losses ceasing entirely, so that the old nightly emissions again commenced, at intervals, and his desires and powers evidently began to return. The administration of my Aphrodisiac Remedy with strict attention to diet, and general hygienic measures, made the improvements still more manifest, but it was necessary for him to abandon *business* altogether, and live perfectly at ease.

In six months he was decidedly *restored,* to a very great extent, though not fully to the condition he enjoyed originally. . . .

In ten months after my seeing him he did marry, and the result was very satisfactory. He is now the happy Father of two healthy children, and in the enjoyment of very tolerable health himself. His sexual powers however are inferior to what they ought to be, and to what they would have been had he married earlier, but still, as he expresses in one of his Letters, sufficient for the mutual happiness of himself and partner. His mind has, to a great extent, recovered its powers, but he is not even now capable of any continued mental efforts, as in former times.

SAVED BY DIET

Fortunately there were cures for lasciviousness just as there were cures for the unhappy results of excessive continence. Sylvester Graham proudly reported how a parent following his regimen, effected treatment of a case of "infantile sexuality."

"I have two little sons [Graham's correspondent wrote], the one about four years old, the other about two.[5] We very early began to accustom them to the use of animal food, and they soon became exceedingly fond of it, and seemed to care little about anything else, if they could get as much flesh as they desired. Not considering it objectionable aliment for children, their mother and myself were disposed to indulge them pretty freely. The health of the elder boy began to be quite delicate, and I was continually filled with anxiety for his life; and indeed, both of them were subject to very frequent turns of indisposition. It has always been our custom to put our children to bed two or three hours before we retired, and when we retired, to take them up and let them urinate, to prevent their wetting the bed. And it was a matter of remark and surprise with us, that when we took them up for this purpose, we *invariably* found them affected with priapism [erection]. Another fact was equally surprising to us; our younger child was very fond of being held in lap, and fondled, and played with by his parents and others with whom he was well acquainted. When in his mother's lap, the little fellow manifested an ardour in hugging and kissing her, which had all the appearance of real wantonness. Indeed, this was often carried so far as actually to embarrass her, when others were present. The same was almost invariably true when he was caressing other females; but when he was in my lap, and hugging or caressing me, or any other gentleman, there were no such indications.

"Now, Sir, the most interesting part of my story is this: Soon after I heard your Lectures, I put my boys on a simple vegetable diet, and have kept them strictly upon it ever since. The result is, that the health of my elder son has much improved, and they both of them now uninterruptedly enjoy the most uniform, excellent health; and when we take them up at nights to urinate, we never find any of the appearances just described. Our younger son is still fond of being in his mother's lap and caressing her, but his priapism on such occasions has entirely disappeared; and we are now perfectly convinced, not only that their former wantonness was caused by their free use of flesh-meat, but that their general health was very injuriously affected by the same cause."

ABSTINENCE IS THE BEST POLICY

Absence of completely effective contraception was only part of the problem facing couples seeking to avoid unwanted pregnancies; they also had to contend with medical advice which condemned their behavior and presented it as a matter for shame, guilt, and contrition.

CASE 1. A man thirty-three years old, of a marked sanguine temperament and athletic frame; eight years married and the father of six children; a cooper, whose pay did not suffice for the necessities of so numerous a family, except by the utmost economy.[6] His measure was full, and a newcomer was undesirable, so the unfortunate fellow took every precaution to ward off so formidable an eventuality, at the same time continuing with the same assiduity his relationships with his wife. He assured us that the preservative means, to which he had recourse, differed in no respect from that which in our time is in general usage, and was of a sort to give him every security. This maneuvering lasted scarcely six months, and there had been no other change in the general habits of this man.

His general condition had undergone no change. His appetite was preserved, and his digestion was as usual in the past. Nevertheless, he grew thin; a slight trembling agitated his frame when in the vertical position, and he was often obliged to stop his work. "Besides," he said, "I perceived myself giddy, and often in the middle of the street I saw the houses turn around me." Nothing in the organic condition of this patient, notwithstanding a very careful examination, being able to enlighten us as to the cause of these grave symptoms, for a moment we thought it might be spermatorrhoea. But after a new examination, we were compelled to reject this diagnosis. We then definitely stopped at an idea, which had, we should avow, seduced us, because it was a new opportunity to verify an opinion which had greatly pre-occupied us—that is to say, that the pathologic condition under observation was owing to a nervous perturbation, caused by abnormal sexual relations [birth control]. . . .

Our whole prescription was limited to the recommendation—not to restore the rights to nature—he might then have demanded of us that we should undertake to support a seventh child, and, as he could not himself raise it, he might have been right—we advised him to observe continence, representing to him the danger to which his present culpable conduct was leading him, and we undertook to indicate to him the resources which hygiene afforded, to diminish the sacrifice which we demanded of his firmness. The advice was faithfully followed; for, hardly two months afterward, we had the satisfaction of seeing the patient, who came to thank us, and we scarcely recognized him, so great was the change of his external appearance. He had regained his *embonpoint,* and he felt no trace of his former troubles.

THE TRAGEDY OF TOO MANY CHILDREN

There were men and women who questioned whether continence was the prime alternative to bearing unwanted children. Among items documenting their belief in birth control was testimony from hapless individuals suffering from miserable marriages or fearing that more offspring would jeopardize health or livelihood. The following letter was addressed to a member of the Oneida Community.

May 12, 1872

I must tell you a sad story.[7] Two years ago last September my daughter was married; the next June she had a son born; the next year in July she had a daughter born; and if nothing happens to prevent she will be confined for the third time in the coming June; that is three times in less than two years. Her children are sickly, and she is sick and discouraged. When she first found she was in the family way this last time, she acted like a crazy person; went to her family physician, and talked with him about having an operation performed. He encouraged her in it, and performed it before she left the office, but without success. She was in such distress that she thought she could not live to get home. I was frightened at her looks, and soon learned what she had done. I tried to reason with her, but found her reason had left her on that subject. She said she never would have this child if it cost her life to get rid of it. After a week she went to the doctor again. He did not accomplish his purpose, but told her to come again in three months. She went at the time appointed in spite of my tears and entreaties. I told her that I should pray that Christ would discourage her; and sure enough she had not courage to try the operation, and came home, but cannot be reconciled to her condition. She does not appear like the same person she was three years ago, and is looking forward with sorrow instead of joy to the birth of her child. I often think if the young women of the [Oneida]

Community could have a realizing sense of the miseries of married life as it is in the world, they would ever be thankful for their home.

Your sincere friend, ———

Alternately inviting pity and psychoanalysis, letters and case histories appearing in nineteenth-century advice manuals have their own ring of truth. Undoubtedly some are distorted, a few may even be total fabrications, but they also contain evidence of what orthodox morality meant in real lives. These stories remind us (as advisers' pious generalities cannot) that moral codes affect human beings, that "miseries of married life," *trials of childbearing, and fears of sexuality are not just abstract formulations.*

---

1 L. N. Fowler, *Marriage: Its History and Ceremonies; With a Phrenological and Physiological Exposition of the Functions and Qualifications for Happy Marriages*, 22nd ed. (New York: Fowlers and Wells, Publishers, 1853), p. 156.

2 Dr. Sylvester Graham, *Chastity, In a Course of Lectures to Young Men; Intended also, for the Serious Consideration of Parents and Guardians* (New York: Fowler and Wells, Publishers, n.d.), p. 50.

3 Ibid., pp. 51–52.

4 Frederick Hollick, *The Male Generative Organs In Health and Disease, from Infancy to Old Age*, 120th ed. [sic.] (New York: T. W. Strong, n.d.), pp. 382–87.

5 Graham, *Chastity*, p. 42.

6 Augustus K. Gardner, *The Conjugal Relationships as Regards Personal Health and Hereditary Well-Being Practically Treated*, 5th ed. (Glasgow: Thomas D. Morison, 1905), pp. 89–91.

7 John Humphrey Noyes, *Male Continence* (Oneida, New York: Office of Oneida Circular, 1872), p. 4.

BIBLIOGRAPHICAL NOTE

"So far no one has attempted to make a bibliographical survey of discussions of sex in American historical writing," John C. Burnham recently observed. This is not the place to break such a firmly established tradition of neglect. Fortunately, Professor Burnham's own "American Historians and the Subject of Sex," *Societas,* II (Autumn 1972), 307–16, is a fine guide to much relevant literature. Yet Burnham did not seek to be comprehensive and he has omitted useful titles, including influential books and articles dealing with Victorian Britain. I have cited some of these in the Introduction, but any serious bibliography must include Keith Thomas, "The Double Standard," *Journal of the History of Ideas,* XXIX (April 1959), 195–216. Also omitted by Burnham are Robert E. Riegel, "Changing American Attitudes Toward Prostitution (1800–1920)," *Journal of the History of Ideas,* XXIX (July 1968), 437–52; John R. Betts, "Mind and Body in Early American Thought," *Journal of American History,* LIV (March 1968), 787–805; and Michael Gordon and M. Charles Bernstein, "Mate Choice and Domestic Life in the Nineteenth-Century Marriage Manual," *Journal of Marriage and Family,* XXXII (November 1970), 665–74. The latter provides both an analysis and a check-list of books like those reproduced in this volume.

There are, in addition, wide-ranging surveys of American sexual attitudes: Sidney Ditzion, *Marriage, Morals, and Sex in America: A History of Ideas* (New York: Bookman Associates, 1953), and Milton Rugoff, *Prudery and Passion* (G. P. Putnam's Sons, 1971). Brief and perceptive are the comments of Oscar Handlin in Chapter VI of *Race and Nationality in American Life* (Boston: Little, Brown & Co., 1957). More limited in scope, David J. Pivar, *Purity Crusade: Sexual Morality and Social Control, 1868–1900* (Westport, Conn.: Greenwood Press, 1973), nevertheless promises to be a significant contribution.

INDEX